INTERSECTIONAL CLASS STRUGGLE

THEORY AND PRACTICE

INTERSECTIONAL CLASS STRUGGLE
THEORY AND PRACTICE

Michael Beyea Reagan

Intersectional Class Struggle: Theory and Practice
© 2021 Michael Reagan
This edition © 2021 AK Press
ISBN 978-1-84935-412-7
E-ISBN 978-1-84935-413-4
Library of Congress Control Number: 2020946157

Published by AK Press and the Institute for Anarchist Studies

AK Press   AK Press
370 Ryan Avenue #100   33 Tower Street
Chico, CA 95973   Edinburgh, EH6, 7BN
USA   Scotland
www.akpress.org   www.akuk.com
akpress@akpress.org   akuk@akpress.org

The addresses above would be delighted to provide you with the latest
AK Press catalog, featuring several thousand books, pamphlets, audio
and video products, and stylish apparel published and distributed
by AK Press. Alternatively, visit our websites for the complete
catalog, latest news and updates, events and secure ordering.

Institute for Anarchist Studies
PO Box 90454
Portland, OR 97290
https://anarchiststudies.org
info@anarchiststudies.org

Cover illustration by Naty Kosloff
Printed in the United States of America on acid-free, recycled paper

For Angela

It is bitter, the bread that has been made by slaves.

—Nicholas Nekrāsoff

Our name is legion though our oppression be great . . . we war with oppression in every form—with rank, save that which merit gives.

—Sarah Bagley

CONTENTS

Preface

Of Ourselves, a New Foundation for Class

When I started working on this project in 2016, the election of billionaire Donald Trump had just hit like a freight train. Social movements that had been winning significant victories in the previous year—such as Black Lives Matter, the Indigenous movement against Keystone XL, Latinx immigrant struggles, and women's movements against sexual violence—were knocked onto a defensive footing and had to adjust to the new terrain. Most analysts who tried to explain the election results looked alternatively to race, class, or gender, often as exclusive frameworks, for the cause. A major facet of the debate was whether it was the racism of voters supporting Trump's xenophobia, or their class interests, as a backlash to 40 years of neoliberalism, which led to Trump's election. Still others framed it as a manifestation of a deeply misogynistic culture not yet ready to elect a woman, Hillary Clinton, his Democratic Party challenger. As with the investigation of a train wreck, scholars, organizers, and analysts picked through the debris of the election to piece together what had just happened.[1]

Class was certainly one component of the election but, as with most things in life, the ultimate causes were complicated. The questions over what explained the rise of Trump and the renewed interest in the role of class, especially the "white working class," is just one example of a class resurgence in our political moment. From the surprise campaigns of Bernie Sanders and Jeremy Corbyn, to laments about the unprecedented wealth inequality of the "second gilded age," to debates over the primacy of class or race by contemporary academics and activists, social class is once again a hot topic. Because it has emerged as one of the more important political dynamics of the twenty-first century, we need to take a moment to better understand what it is that we are talking about when we speak of class: What is it? Why is it often connected to conflict and struggle? What is the working class? And why are class analysis and movements of the working class seeing a resurgence right now? To answer these questions, *Intersectional Class Struggle* argues that social class is defined by the difference and variety of us, regular working people, in our everyday lives. In the last analysis, class is made of ourselves.

Intersectional

Despite the interest, much of the contemporary debate about class is impoverished, and Trump's election is no exception. In the social train wreck that the election revealed, using isolated pieces of wreckage from the crash, the analysis that people drew was only partial. Was it race, or class, or gender that best explained the social crisis? This was simply the wrong question to ask; the obvious answer was "yes." Unfortunately, this fractured perspective framed virtually the entirety of the mainstream debate with arguments based on exclusive and essential race or class explanations. To understand each social factor as distinct, rather than a complex whole of the "social totality," in which race, class, and gender (along with immigration, disability, colonialism, and other vectors of social power) were mutually reinforcing social phenomena, was part of the problem. But more than this, the language and ideas used to discuss class were particularly poor, alternatively viewing level of education or income and tax register as an analytic stand-in for class. At the core of the problem of discussing class was an inability to define it.

One helpful corrective is the concept of intersectionality. Trump ran specifically on class issues, or, shall we say, a particular articulation of white working-class masculinity was at the foundation of his campaign. He used the language of class to speak directly to "wage earners." He fostered racial fear by telling audiences that "they" (immigrants) "are taking our jobs, they're taking our manufacturing jobs.

They're taking our money. They're killing us." His record of abuse of women fit into a pattern of patriarchal violence and braggadocio. The odiousness of a figure such as Trump is hard to face, but even harder to understand are the motivations of his supporters, who are also often the targets of his violence. Despite the offensive and harmful language he used about women, a majority of white women voted for Trump. And he won their vote despite facing sexual assault allegations and running against the first major-party woman presidential nominee.[2]

Demonstrating the need for intersectional analysis, in the complex phenomenon of the Trump election, a greater percentage of Latinx voters cast their ballot for Trump than for Mitt Romney, whose father was from México. Although Black voters supported Democrats in overwhelming numbers, more stayed away from the polls in 2016 with Clinton as the candidate than any election in a decade. Of those who bothered voting, a greater percentage of Black voters supported Trump than the Republican candidate in 2012. And if we look at non-voters, tens of millions completely stayed away from the polls. Many of these non-voters were both culturally and structurally what we can call "working class." This basic divide in the political arena, a class divide, reveals the degree to which class and its intersections with race and gender influenced the election and the political institutions of our time.[3]

However, to look at any one of these factors—gender separate from race separate from class—without considering them in all in their totality leaves us with a diminished understanding of social power and oppression. If we think about how these factors intersect, how particular sets of interests are articulated in particular historical moments, not only will our understanding be improved but so too our movements for liberation.

Class

In this book, I argue that class can help us understand these apparent contradictions. In much of the work on intersectionality, however, the thinking about class is not robust. This is in part because the tradition of intersectional theory tended to under-theorize class, as I explain more in the introduction. This poor footing has had spillover effects into our movements today and our analysis of contemporary events. In the election debate, depending on how one defined class— by education or income—very different explanations came forward. For those who saw education as a defining factor, Trump's election was the "revenge of the white working class," in which those with less education voted in increasing numbers for Trump. Others argued that Trump's support from working-class voters was a "myth," that it largely came from middling business owners and that his voters were "better off economically compared to most Americans." Trump contributed to this confusion, equating working-class interests to "protect jobs" with the white supremacist fear of immigrants, and a particular brand of violent and reactive masculinity.[4]

Unfortunately, this equation of working-class interests with whiteness wasn't limited to Trump. In his rejection of reparations and insistence on increasing police funding in the wake of the 2020 Black Lives Matter uprisings, candidate Bernie Sanders also demonstrated a construction of "working-class" interests with "white" interests. This is not to equate these two very different politicians; Sanders is a politician on the other side of the political universe from Trump, with a long history of anti-racist activism. I point to Sanders's weaknesses on race to demonstrate that our political understanding of class needs some serious work, even for the best of us on the left. Focusing on programs to establish "universal" working-class standards from the harm of American capitalism is laudable and would provide great relief for working-class people of color. But color-blind policies cannot adequately address the difference and diversity to be found in the American working class or the historic inequities that affect Black America. If class is made "of ourselves," then we need to reflect the variety of working-class experience in our class politics.[5]

* * *

At the end of working on *Intersectional Class Struggle*, I found myself writing during the combined impacts of the coronavirus disease (COVID-19) pandemic and the unprecedented movement power of Black Lives Matter in 2020. Albeit powerful, attempting to look strictly at "class" factors to explain this moment gets us in trouble.

For example, the COVID-19 crisis has exacerbated the already gross wealth inequality in the United States; the richest and most powerful tech corporations have ballooning stock valuations and profitability propped up by government spending and guarantees for the rich. A study by the Institute for Policy Studies found, in the first three months of the crisis in the United States, the nation's billionaires increased their wealth by over $600 billion, bringing their total assets to $3.5 trillion, more than the total wealth for the entire U.S. Latinx population. In the same period, more than 44 million people had to file for unemployment relief because they lost their jobs and, by mid-2020, 40 million were facing eviction, all disproportionately affecting people of color. Amazon's stock valuation soared during the crisis to $1.5 trillion, doubling its profit during the pandemic and bringing in a record $5.2 billion in revenue. Jeff Bezos, Amazon's chief executive officer (CEO) and already the richest person in the world, gained $13 billion in one day on a stock surge, his personal value up $70 billion on the year to roughly $180 billion while the real economy suffered. Meanwhile, Amazon workers who make that profit possible were being called in to work, getting infected with COVID-19, and dying. By May, there were eight known deaths. When workers protested those conditions, they were fired.[6]

Outside the tech industry, similar patterns emerged. "Essential workers," those in the front lines of COVID-19 exposure (e.g., grocery workers, medical aides, transit and logistics workers) are disproportionately workers of color, and disproportionately dying. While the stock market boomed on a speculative frenzy, and Trump urged the economy to reopen, working people were dying in the tens of thousands. Income was a strong corollary for COVID-19 fatalities, as these were typically workers without sick time and who were not able to afford health care. They were also people of color. Black mortality from COVID-19 was six times higher than whites aged 45–54, and ten times higher for those aged 35–44. And men were a larger number of COVID-19 deaths than women, with more Black men facing hospitalizations. These death rates under COVID-19 are on top of the "preexisting condition" of racialized health inequality under capitalism and white supremacy. According to Harvard scholars, U.S. "health disparities between blacks and whites run deep," with African Americans more likely to have diabetes, hypertension, and heart disease than whites. Black children die from asthma at a 500% greater rate than white children. All before this crisis.[7]

Besides the pain, compassion, and quest for justice this should inspire in our hearts, it quickly becomes clear that when we talk about class in this society, in inequality and mortality, we must rapidly move to an intersectional understanding with race, gender, and other social factors. If we hope to have a better understanding of our current moment and our very recent history, we need better analytic tools to help us navigate the complexity of our world and hopefully build for a more humane future.

Struggle

The final aim of this work is to restore a tradition of liberation and emancipation to class politics today. From the origins of the intersectional class-struggle tradition that we explore, emancipation has been a core tenet of the movement. Conceptions of self-emancipation—the idea that better futures are possible, but only if we make them happen ourselves—have been driving motivators of class politics for centuries. Many would point to the writings of the International Workingmen's [sic] Association in the nineteenth century, the so-called First International, for the origin of this idea. The First International, of which the revolutionary thinker Karl Marx was a significant contributor, understood that "the emancipation of the workers must be accomplished by the workers themselves." They believed, in short, that from the horrors of capitalism, no one will free us but ourselves. "Workers of the world unite," goes a popularization of Marx's words, "you have nothing to lose but your chains." Freedom, deliverance, liberation—that the movement of working people contains an ideal of human emancipation as part of class politics is a major intervention of this book.[8]

It is very revealing, however, that the concept of self-emancipation present in Marx and the European labor movement comes from the Atlantic world tradition of the abolition of slavery; it is rooted in Black liberation. If we pause to think about it, there is no better example of the emancipation of labor than the successful revolts of enslaved people of the eighteenth and nineteenth centuries. Before

Marx, "self-emancipation" was the phrase of a romantic poet, Lord Byron, and it motivated the spirit of liberation in the Anglo-American abolitionist world. For "hereditary bondsmen" (enslaved people), Byron writes that those "who would be free themselves must strike the blow." One's liberation can only come from self-activity, he argues. That phrase became a slogan of nineteenth-century abolitionists, a favorite of Frederick Douglass, and its truth was borne out in an unfolding history of liberation—the Haitian revolution, the St. John uprising, the Malê revolts of enslaved people, and other collective emancipations. After the end of slavery in the American Civil War, the example of Black liberation inspired many others to strive for the seemingly impossible. It is perhaps no coincidence that the International Workingmen's Association and Marx's *Capital* both were launched in the wake of Black Americans' freedom struggle. According to historian David Roediger, the revolutionary and liberatory example of American slaves' self-emancipation fueled other movements of the nineteenth century, including labor, women's liberation, national liberation, Indigenous sovereignty, and many more.[9]

That the concept of self-emancipation is frequently credited to European thinkers, rather than the Black collective experience, is indicative of the ways white supremacy distorts our own history and movements. At the same time, it tells us something more: that movements seep into one another, that liberation is infectious, and that collective liberation has been a core part of working-class struggle from the origins of the modern period—slavery and wage labor included. In short, working people have struggled for an ideal of human emancipation that transcends incremental material improvement and parochial interests. These visions of liberation are part and parcel of class politics. As we develop movements for collective liberation in our own time with the reemergence of the Black Lives Matter movement, we need to hold dear the legacy and vision of self-emancipation. Whereas Trump and his backers provide one kind of articulation of the working class, we must provide another.

* * *

If we return to our initial question about what defines class, we need to look at the complex, contradictory, and intersectional nature of class experience for answers. Therefore, this work explores questions of structure and agency, of subjectivity and definition, of class studies and movement practice. Rather than liberal constructions of "them," over there, the working class, or Marx's notion of "it," as in a "class for itself," we argue for a new articulation of class based on our complex and contradictory collective experience. By taking a historical approach, we see working people ourselves are both agents and subjects of social forces. Agents, in that when we organize, rebel, revolt, and reject the structures of exploitation and oppression, we can create something new, new social relationships and institutions that contribute to a different future. Subjects in that we inherit from the past the traditions of property, poverty, white supremacy, patriarchy, and colonialism that structure our disempowerment in the here and now. This framing is part of the definition that I use for this book. Regarding the working class, we are the ones who compose the class: our experiences and our relationships, we as teachers, as laborers, office workers, homemakers, parents, victims of police brutality, refugees, and migrants—us. Class structures our lives, and we are its living embodiment. When we speak of class, we are speaking of ourselves.

It is from here that this book takes its starting point. I hope to offer an introductory guide to the major ideas of the intersectional class-struggle tradition for today's activists, organizers, students, and scholars. More than this, I hope this book will be a useful weapon in the class war from the bottom. As I write, the fate of the planet and humankind is in a bad way; Trump's election and the COVID-19 crisis revealed the wreckage around us. And although he was defeated in the 2020 election, the conditions that produced Trump's presidency are still with us. Threats to our very existence are real and growing more ominous by the day. The source of many of these problems—from catastrophic global climate change, the increasing threat of nuclear confrontation, and the rise of hate groups, the far-right, and neo-fascist movements in countries around the world—is rooted in capitalism, in the exploitation, alienation, and dehumanization that is inherent in the process of capitalist profit and expansion. If we hope to survive, capitalism must be undone, and this is a process that cannot happen without class struggle, without working people, us, deciding to create something better. That we have seen moments of this type of transformation even in our very recent history gives me great hope. This work is an attempt to make some small contribution to those efforts.

—MBR, Seattle, Washington, August 2020

Acknowledgments

It is often thought that scholarship is a lonely endeavor. But it is not true. A book such as this is truly a collective effort; writing it has taught me the meaning of communal nature behind all work. This is particularly so for the many activists and theorists of which this work is a synthesis. A major contribution came from my students of labor studies at the University of Washington in Tacoma and Seattle. Teaching labor studies with working-class students and the pressures, questions, and insights they brought to our class sessions are fundamental parts of what makes up this work. I owe them a debt of thanks.

I'd also like to thank my wonderful editors at the Institute for Anarchist Studies (IAS), Chris Dixon and Tamara Myers. They have stuck with this project for the long haul and truly believed in the importance of the intervention throughout. They've also helped at each crucial decision point and helped to carry me through some difficult periods. Chris and Tamara provided detailed and thoughtful comments on many (too many) drafts, and they made this work unquestionably stronger with their questions, insights, and careful attention. I owe them a very large debt. To Kristian Williams, who worked on the logistics of the publishing and contract with me at IAS, and on improving the caliber of this and other works, I also owe thanks. And thanks also to Paul and Lara Messersmith-Glavin for their movement scholarship and support through the IAS.

The collective staff at AK, particularly Suzanne Shaffer, Charles Weigl, and Zach Blue, I owe a big thanks. Especially to Charles, for helping me understand the process of the publishing world and the importance of getting titles right. I thank the excellent copy editor, Jude Ortiz. Also, to the readers who agreed to write support for this project, especially Noam Chomsky, Dean Spade, Kali Akuno, Tithi Bhattacharya, Paul Ortiz and the others too numerous to mention, thank you. The political work of Professor Chomsky in particular has been a big influence on this project. To the wonderful artist Naty Kos, thanks for the beautiful illustration for the cover.

Many comrades, scholars, and organizers helped me think through material in this work, and to you I owe gratitude. The wonderful Sharmeen Khan wrote a very thoughtful review and provided comments. Her points of support were precise, and her comments of criticism were sharp—but they all made this work stronger. Romina Akemi read through an early version and provided very helpful and thorough comments, at a time when the manuscript did not deserve that level of attention and during which she was already very busy with her dissertation work. Jessica Molly Moran and Thomas Makay both pointed me in the direction of useful sources and scholarship on anarchism and critiques of materialism. Thanks to Adrienne Elise for her research aid and access to helpful online resources. My comrades in struggle, Pablo Abufom, JM Wong, Kurtis Dengler, Jessica Ramirez, Carlos Perez, Barbara Madeloni, and Dean Chaim all provided examples of hope in struggle and many conversations about how we create a better world. Adam Weaver is a conscientious and thoughtful comrade whose read of the work helped it improve. To Wayne Price, whose principled and very direct comments helped to advance some loose conceptual work in earlier versions, my thanks. Washington State labor historians Trevor Griffey and Mike Honey both provided comments and thoughtful criticism and encouragement. To Michael Noonan, my lifelong friend, comrade, and model of intellectual and working-class scholar, many thanks for comments and attempts to prevent me from making grave errors. Sebastian Lopez Vergara read through an early version, introduced me to the work of Stuart Hall, and is the kind of loving comrade I hope to be some day. Andrew Hedden did serious work on my drafts and encouraged reframing to make the work better at every stage. Laura Martin,

Marianne Garneau, Angela Malorni, Jessie Kindig, Miguel Chevere, Tom Wetzel, Jen Rogue, Morgan Rose, Garret Shishido Strain, David Spataro, Matthew Van Duyn, Dan Berger, and Moon Ho Jung: I owe thanks to all. And to my most immediate movement comrades and some of my most beloved people, Isabelle Tetu, Helena Ribero, Grace Reinke, Riddhi Mehta-Neugebauer, and Kara Sweidel, many thanks.

I also owe thanks to the faculty, grad students, and staff in the Departments of History and Political Science at the University of Washington, and to the social science divisions at the University of Washington, Tacoma. I gained a lot from my time there. Although an academic job is not one of them. The skills, training, and support from the dedicated scholars in those departments was formative.

Thanks to my family, my mom and dad, who have supported me throughout this work, and my sister, who in many ways has been a crucial voice of support and love for me in these years; and to my friends and community who continually lift me up.

And, in the last, to Angela, learning to love and heal with you is some of the hardest work I've ever done. But some of the most rewarding and generative. I'm forever grateful for your patience, hard work, love, and support in life through this project.

Introduction

There's strength in organization. There's no way any
individual can accomplish very much. You've got to have
strength . . . coming out the Depression, everybody was in
the same boat, and realized it. When you're catching hell
together, sometimes you see eye to eye a little better.

—Clarence Coe

Clarence Coe, the grandson of slaves, was a Black factory worker at
the Memphis Firestone tire factory in the mid–twentieth century.[1]
Growing up in rural Tennessee, he witnessed the violence of white supremacy firsthand. At a young age, he saw "the results of a lynching
or two" and more regular assaults and humiliations, such as watching
Black residents get kicked as they walked down the street or others
attacked by white boys at a parade. As an adult, he left for the city of
Memphis only to find that the same structures of white supremacy
met him there. Employers segregated jobs and paid African-American
workers less than whites; and white co-workers attacked Black workers, slashing Coe's tires and once attempting to beat him to death for
violating the strictures of white supremacy. In that incident, in which
Coe was stabbed and nearly lost his life, he was targeted for trying
to build a union at a Sealy mattress factory. Luckily, he fought back
with a wooden post to save himself; in this case, he was fighting for

unionization and running into the structures of white supremacy and racist violence. From Coe's experience, then, it emerges that unionization and building worker solidarity was an important facet of the struggle against white supremacy and for collective Black liberation. Coe's experiences and ideas, and others like them, are at the core of the intersectional class-struggle tradition.[2]

Coe was explicit about this connection—the necessity of the class struggle to Black liberation and the importance of interracial struggle for collective liberation. Coe told his interviewer in 1996 that, even in the 1990s, "You have white folks who still believe they can make it without us, they can make it without organization." Instead, he argued it was important to "revive the union spirit" and that this struggle was "going to take a long pull. You're going to have to go back to the basics, get some of these young whites and young blacks together and start organizing, and the races stand together." Here and in the epigraph presented earlier, Coe is expressing the tenets of intersectional class struggle, the idea that, despite significant differences, most of us are "in the same boat" and can come to recognize it. White workers can't make it without Black liberation. From Coe's lifelong experience as an organizer in his union, in the National Association for the Advancement of Colored People (NAACP), and in his church, the best way to address social oppression was the union, through collective organization and action. Coe's expression of intersectional class consciousness is remarkable but is by no means unique; his insights are in fact part of a long tradition that takes the issues of race, class, and gender oppression and exploitation seriously. They are part of a synthetic whole that must be struggled against holistically, collectively, if we want to create a better world free from exploitation and oppression.[3]

This book is about the tradition of intersectional class struggle. Less a coherent doctrine, school of thought, or movement practice, intersectional class struggle is found at the margins of myriad social movements, in individual rebels and radicals, and in social theorists and rank-and-file militants. Looking at patterns from contemporary and historical social movements, there is nonetheless enough coherence and consistency of ideas, analysis, and practice to identify and delimit a rough tradition of intersectional class struggle. From voices within the Black freedom movement, unionized workers, working-class feminists, LGBTQ+ liberation struggles, and climate organizers, the intersectional class-struggle tradition embeds the fight against all forms of exploitation and oppression within anti-capitalist struggle. This tradition sees in the fight to end racism and patriarchy the seeds of a liberatory struggle that must also undo capitalism and class if it hopes to live up to the promise of human emancipation. My argument is that intersectional class analysis is as diverse and far-reaching as the working-class people that it comes from. Indeed, because class composition is made up of us—in all our great variety and difference—our struggles, and our hopes and desires, the intersectional class-struggle tradition represents a broad vision for a liberatory future and therefore must take up a broad spectrum of social and political issues. Coe and others discussed in this work may be somewhat unique, but they are not alone. Together, these voices compose the workings of a tradition of class struggle and intersectional organizing that has articulated a boundless vision of human emancipation.

Despite the vibrancy of this tradition, there are figures in social movements and on the left who argue that the salience of class has diminished in the twenty-first century. For them, class analysis grew out of the experience of white workers in large-scale industrial production or social theorists removed from the realities of social struggle. It therefore cannot offer current movements a viable framework for navigating contemporary social and political developments or a strategy to move forward. These voices are strongest on the left, surprisingly, and argue that the politics and theory of class struggle reflect a unique historical moment, that the working class is now in decline, and that class-struggle politics are no longer relevant. For example, in the 1980s, the French theorist André Gorz argued that, with the failure of proletarian revolutions and the growth of automation, the time of the working class as a revolutionary subject was over. In *Farewell to the Working Class*, Gorz writes that "the disappearance of the polyvalent skilled worker" because of automation "has also entailed the disappearance of the class able to take charge of the socialist project and translate it into reality." In short, for Gorz and others like him, class struggle and the working class were phenomena of the past.[4]

Numerous social theorists grew up in the wake of Gorz and offer similar arguments that class, especially the working class, is no longer relevant in the way it once was. Guy Standing, for example, argues that the working class is over because their employment is far more precarious now than it was previously. The new class, the "precariat," is part of a more stratified class system that diminishes the importance of the traditional working class. Others, such as Michael Hardt and Antonio Negri, accept the decline of the working class as they look for new revolutionary subjects, what they call the "multitude" or the "mass," as more potent ground for revolutionary struggle. What all these approaches share is a turn away from the working class as a revolutionary subject and class as an important analytic for contemporary politics.[5]

These critiques miss the mark. Although there are important and ongoing changes to the nature of work under capitalism and the composition of the working class in the twenty-first century, class, class struggle, and the working class are still very much alive. What the critics miss is historical understanding of the working class that shows that precarity and class composition (the process of building class consciousness in particular historical circumstances) have always been factors of class struggle and that currently there are more working-class people, even engaged in industrial production, than at any other point in human history. In the United States and other industrialized countries, we are entering a "second gilded age" in which tremendous wealth inequity and class conflict over austerity and state policy are the leading characteristics of the era. Wages, property, and profit still rule our economy, politics, and society, and so the structures and consciousness of class are as present as ever.[6]

But this is not a return to "class reductionism," the wrongheaded notion that all social struggles are based in the more fundamental role of class, and that questions of racial or gender oppression are secondary to the class struggle. There is a tradition, mostly from a branch of Marxism, that argues that class is paramount and that addressing other social struggles distracts from what should be our main focus—class struggle. For example, Melvin Leiman, in his *Political Economy of Racism*, argues that "class is the more fundamental category; class stratification is a necessary feature of capitalist society, while racial stratification is only one possible form." He goes on to conclude that "the race question ultimately [is] only part of the class question." Leiman has a sympathetic view of anti-racist struggle, arguing that movements for Black liberation should be wholeheart-edly embraced by socialist revolutionaries as moving toward interra-cial working-class solidarity. But his class fundamentalism is faulty; racism and white supremacy are not just possible but also extant and are virtually universal in capitalist societies. Further, race and gender have their own dynamics. And class also has a cultural composition, making any singular or "scientific" notion of working-class interests an impossibility. This book presents a different notion of class. It is not that all forms of social struggle are mere facets of the class strug-gle, it is that class is a fundamental component of society and infused and intersectional with virtually all we do.[7]

A core tenet of Leiman's branch of Marxism is that class has a structural component different from other forms of social oppression. For example, G. A. Cohen, in his work, *Karl Marx's Theory of History*, finds the emphasis on culture and consciousness in class formation faulty for this reason. More recently, the work of Vivek Chibber and others in the *Catalyst* journal is to revive "a vital tradition of materi-alist class analysis," and this fits within this brand of Marxism. Chib-ber argues that, although cultural interpretations may work for causal forces in some instances, this is not the case for class. He sees class as a special case because class represents a "kind of structural coer-cion" not present in other forms in society because, in waged work, for the proletarian, one either eats or starves. Consequently, for Chib-ber, whereas cultural theory retains important value in other social forms, class becomes a kind of special case, materially determined more so than other social forms. But by posing culture and structure as distinct social factors, Chibber misses the complex interpenetra-tion of culture and materiality. As we try to argue here, culture has a "structure" of its own, material structure is inherently cultural, and this relationship is at the core of intersectionality.[8]

Intersectional Class Struggle then argues something different from these thinkers: class is structural—but it is both materially and cultur-ally constructed. Race and gender oppression also have their own dy-namics of material and cultural components that form the systems of oppression and exploitation that we experience today. These systems intersect with and support one another, and it is difficult to imagine any one without the others. Those who see class as the most funda-mental form of social organization, exploitation, and oppression are wrong. Instead, a more nuanced understanding of the complex social phenomena of class and the working class as material, cultural, racial, and gendered is important if we are to understand ourselves and our world.

But neither is this work an uncritical embrace of "intersectional" politics. The academic origins of intersectionality are to be found in the writing of legal scholar Kimberlé Crenshaw. Her work, especially the article, "Mapping the Margins: Intersectionality, Identity Politics, and Violence against Women," was groundbreaking for pushing back against the essentialized, reductive, and siloed ways identity was used in the wake of the civil rights movement. Particularly strong in her work, and in Black feminist thought explored later in this book, is her discussion of "difference" in relation to social structures of power. She argues that racism and sexism are inseparable in the lived experience of women and that therefore the way Black women or white women experiences domestic violence is different based on the particular intersections of their experiences. Crenshaw's focus on just two vectors of analysis—race and gender—in her discussion of domestic violence, however, is a major shortcoming of her work. Class is also an important determinant of domestic violence, as women's access to paid work, property, or external resources and support is class-determined and affects their experience of intimate violence. Even more, the entire field and practice of law is based on using violence to protect property. It is inherently a class-defined structure that escapes the critique of Crenshaw and her intersectional framework. Relegating class to the margins of her analysis meant that the foundations of intersectional theory was left with a deficit from which it has struggled to recover; many of the contemporary usages of intersectionality remain focused on race and gender, with class receiving poor theoretical and strategic attention.[9]

This book hopes to correct these oversights; it is about a lived tradition of class struggle. As such, it is not revivification of the subset of Marxists that believes in "class-only" politics, or that class is defined solely by "material" social relationships and can be "scientifically" known. It is also not an argument that class is reducible to a type of social identity, like other types of identity formation, something that is contingent on individual subjectivity but somehow also universal to those who identify as the working class. Instead, it is an attempt to point out that class is an important, complex, and ongoing social phenomenon, and that the intersectional class-struggle tradition infuses movements and politics from the origins of modern capitalism to the present. With modifications, we can retain the powerful insights of materialist analysis and understand that culture is a structural component as much as the institutions of the law or economy. This renewed vision improves our understanding of intersectionality as both material and cultural. It makes for the continued salience of class analysis and the working class, including all our difference, as a political category. We argue here that class remains politically salient, that class struggle is happening all around us, and that building working-class power is an essential ingredient for liberatory movements today.

* * *

There are two ideas that guide the intervention of *Intersectional Class Struggle*. First is a more robust and refined definition of class that builds on the materialist tradition. In this definition, class is about social relationships, about collective interests and the differences between groups, particularly as they relate to property and wages. Whether we get our income and site our primary economic activity in ownership or in wages is a key class determinant. But it is more than this. Class is just as much how people identify and understand themselves and the world, and how they think about the social relationships that define them. Class is therefore a mix of "material" and "cultural" factors. Material factors are things that are tangible, can be touched, or have a relationship to the material world. For example, economic structures such as wages and property are considered material. Cultural factors are things that are generated in the mind, things such as ideology, language, or assumed social practices and systems of meaning. Part of what we hope to demonstrate, however, is that these two analytic categories dramatically affect one another and might not be as separate as they first appear. It is in this complex mix of factors that class formation happens, that people come to articulate their role and their relationships, construct expectations, and take action to further their collective interests. This is a process we call class composition.[10]

Second, we argue that class is fundamentally intersectional. This is to say that class is not the "core" or the "major" social determinant that is modified through race or gender like a prefix. Instead, race, class, gender, ability, and other social forms are fundamentally co-determinative and co-constitutive. The structures that shape class also shape race and gender, and those social categories are just as much material and cultural as is class. This is especially true when we get away from abstract social categories and think about lived experience. When Black workers are the last hired and first fired, and face unemployment rates twice as high as whites, this is undoubtedly about racism. It is also a function of class, about labor-market competition, exploitation, and work. For those trapped with a violent partner because they can't leave for fear of destitution, this is unquestionably about structures of patriarchy. But it also about economic inequality and independence and the structural role women play in our economy. Therefore, in our lived experience, we perceive the analytic categories of race, class, and gender as inseparable. Intersectionality sees social phenomena as a mix of the material and the cultural, in which the parts complement one another, or intersect, in the lived experiences of the social whole. This is true too for forms of social power and oppression, in which race, class, and gender overlap and support each other in their construction and operation.[11]

To illustrate how we understand class as material, cultural, and intersectional, let's consider the example of homelessness. At its core, homelessness is a material condition—someone doesn't have access to shelter. It is also related to other material factors, economic factors, such as unemployment, wages too low to pay for housing, lack of access to the necessary means of subsistence, lack of property, speculative housing markets, or medical expenses and bankruptcy. But each of these are social relationships; people lack secure property, or may be isolated from friends or family who could provide care, or lack state programs as an ultimate fallback. Their housing problems might be enhanced by race and gender, as African Americans continue to face discrimination in rental and mortgage markets or as one in five trans people have experienced homelessness. These questions are exacerbated by the individual values of those exposed to homelessness, including internalized stigma that mark some as "undeserving," and suggest that asking for help is a source of shame.

Others may reject the paternalism that often comes with nonprofit-organized social services for the homeless, or make other choices and hold other values that in part contribute to their condition of homelessness. And so, in addition to being an economic and material question, this is a cultural question, a demonstration of the individual and collective values a society expresses. Here materiality, culture, race, class, and gender all come together in a singular experience of homelessness made up of many different component parts and many difference experiences.

With this understanding of the complex interplay between material and cultural factors and intersectionality, we can see how race, class, gender, and sexuality are co-constructed and mutually reinforcing in the structure of our society. Social structures are the institutions and organizations that give a society its particular form and character. For example, wages and markets are some of the structures that define modern capitalism. If we take the labor market as an example, we can see the structural co-composition of race, gender, and class. When we work for wages, we are entering a labor market in which competition is the primary mechanism to determine wages. Competition means that the more workers there are available for a job, the lower the price of the wage that the employer pays to the worker. With lots of workers and few jobs, the employer can set the price as low as the lowest amount any one worker is willing to take. If workers want to get their wages up, they need to restrict market access to those jobs—they need to prevent others from getting access to employment, and thus increase their market value.

There are many possible ways to create labor-market exclusions, and this process demonstrates the utility of intersectional analysis. For example, unions limit competition, in that, if union membership is a requirement for employment, it restricts the market access of other workers, thus raising their wages. But there are others, including structural exclusions that prevent Black workers, immigrants, Muslim workers, women workers, or others from getting access to jobs. With whole sectors of the working class removed from competition, the workers who have the best jobs can come to feel entitled to those positions. They can look for justifications to exclude other workers, immigrants, for example, or anyone who might pose a threat to their competitiveness on the labor market. They can then begin to see difference not as part of the variety of human bodies, cultures, and experiences but as essentialized and permanent markers of inferiority or lack of deservedness. In short, they come to racialize social difference as a defense mechanism against the competitiveness of the labor market. Here the structures of capitalism reinforce the structures of white supremacy and patriarchy, and vice versa. In fact, they are embedded in the same social structure—labor-market competition.

With an intersectional and structural understanding of society, we have better understanding of the kinds of social ills before us and, more importantly, how to better struggle against them. This structural and intersectional understanding of race, class, and gender helps us see the experiences and social conditions that someone like Coe struggled against. For him, the union was a potential mechanism to break down racial exclusions in the structure of the labor market. This is intersectional class struggle. But this analysis also helps explains other social phenomena, much uglier ones, such as why unions have such a long history of supporting white supremacy and xenophobia, for example. Or why anti-immigrant sentiment is a perennial winner for far-right electoral campaigns. It helps us understand the two-tiered labor market of "pink-collar" work and why women are paid less than men. The structural and intersectional understanding that comes from an agile class analysis can help us understand the material and cultural components of race and patriarchy. If, as Karl Marx argued, class is a social relationship based in material conditions, then so too are race and gender social relations based in materiality. What we hope to contribute is an understanding of the interpenetration of culture in all these forces. Indeed, as intersectional theory stresses, to think about these social phenomena as distinct is faulty; they are part of a social whole that we need to understand in its totality if we care to take on any one of these issues.

And whither the working class? Some may argue that, with this more nuanced and complex vision of class, the salience of class politics, and in particular the role of the working class, is diminished. We say no. *Intersectional Class Struggle* argues that the politics of the working class, of those who don't own but who labor, are just as important as ever. We have collective interests different from the ownership class; in fact, our interests are fundamentally at odds, as ownership entitles one to usurpation and exploitation. This is true even for those who don't work, or aren't working now, by nature of their social relationship to property rather than their current employment status.[12] Class then is defined by all of us, in all varieties of occupations, all walks of life, and all cultural backgrounds. It is mediated through myriad social relationships, experiences, and understandings, different based on race, gender, and the other factors discussed here. This diversity within the definition of class means there is no universal class experience, politics, or interests but a multiplicity of working-class voices, perspectives, and priorities. In this, it's hard to find a singular working class, one unitary or "objective" set of criteria that gives us an objective "it," the working class. As we try to argue, there is no "it," there is just us, in all our messy, complex, and contradictory experiences. Here we note a running tension throughout this book—there is no singular or universal working class but a collection of different lives and perspectives, with just one shared element—the struggle against exploitation by property and wages, and thus for human emancipation. Although universalism is abandoned, we still share a core defining structural characteristic: exclusion from property that defines us as working class. In this new definition, we are left with the understanding of class that is simply made of ourselves.[13]

* * *

To explore these themes, this book is divided into three sections: experience, theory, and practice. The first section of the book starts with us, the experience of working-class peoples ourselves. In chapter 1, "Experience," we show how, at the very origins of the wage-labor system, workers developed a far-sighted and transformative vision of how work and society should be organized. They fundamentally rejected the wage system as wage slavery, because of the loss of control of one's labor, and tied their interest to undoing capitalist property relations. In the United States, women were the first industrial workforce, and they saw the wage system as fundamentally tied to patriarchy in that both were systems of control that kept them from being fully free. It is no wonder that early working-class feminist Sarah Bagley declared, for "factory girls" like herself, "We war with oppression in every form—with rank, save that which merit gives." This chapter shows the diversity of the working-class experience through the prism of gender but also the shared critique of capitalism as incompatible with freedom and self-determination.[14]

Chapter 2, "Slavery and Wages," explores the similarities and differences of wage- and slave-labor systems, and the lasting legacy of white supremacy in work today. Slavery divided and defined workers by race, and made systems of labor exploitation comparable to those of industrial capitalism. Today we live in a segregated labor market, in which collectively Black workers are relegated to the worst jobs and racism pays social and cultural rewards to those with white skin. In this picture, Black workers such as Irene Branch and Lillian Roberts saw collective economic gains, and particularly their unions, as agents of civil rights, their vehicles for liberation. This chapter shows that class has several fundamental structural characteristics that transcend the particularities of place, legacy, and subjectivity. At the same time, class is forever infused with gender and race formation, the very particularities of place, history, and culture. That both are true does not diminish class as an analytic. Indeed, this complicated understanding of class struggle, developed by workers themselves, is fundamental to the larger project of human emancipation.

From here, *Intersectional Class Struggle* moves into its second section, on social theory, and explores the theory of class as it has emerged from the seventeenth century to today. It argues that intersectional theory is enhanced by a better understanding of material and cultural factors. Although in reality we can't really separate these forces so neatly, by understanding the mutual co-construction of economy and culture we can see how race, class, and gender are similarly co-determinative. Chapter 3, "Materialism," discusses the "material" understanding of class based in the leading theories of political economy. Starting with John Locke, liberal justifications of property and the capitalist state are based on the labor theory of value that imagines workers enjoying the fruits of their toil. But as working-class movements have pointed out, this is not the reality of capitalism or private property. Instead, workers toil while owners profit. French philosopher Pierre-Joseph Proudhon argued that the problem was property itself, that property was exclusive and created a fundamental divide in society. This is the basis of the class divide, a cleavage founded in ownership that runs through virtually all modern societies, although with variation. It was the German philosopher

Karl Marx who said that the fundamental relationship of class was a material one, between an individual and the "means of production," and between the working and owning classes.

Marx's insights were profound, but he likely erred in how closely he tied class to materiality and excluded other factors. In chapter 4, "Culture," we look at thinkers in the socialist tradition, Marxist and not, who pointed this out. Culture, consciousness, ideology, all took on greater weight as revolutionaries began to think about how to further class struggle with an improved understanding of class formation. For people such as anarchist Rudolph Rocker or Marxist E. P. Thompson, materialist understandings of class simply could not explain the complex lived realities of workers' politics, social formations, and social movements. Another theorist, Stuart Hall, showed us how culture itself can be a "structure" and how it often works to "determine" the material world by shaping our conceptions at a fundamental level. By introducing culture and consciousness into the conversation, they showed that how we, the working class, think about and understand our world and our relationship to other classes is as fundamentally important to class formation as are material factors.

With this insight, a great conceptual leap forward, other thinkers pushed those ideas further still, and chapter 5, "Intersectionality," shows how a material and cultural framework is helpful for intersectional theory. In the "Black radical tradition," theorists such as W. E. B. Du Bois, C. L. R. James, and Cedric Robinson found that race and class formation were indelibly tied. If capitalism and racism both had material and cultural components, then both were ever-present in the other's structure and composition, a process that Robinson called "racial capitalism." Virtually simultaneously, working-class feminists such as Silvia Federici and Selma James drew similar conclusions: women's social oppression and the structures of patriarchy were fused and rooted in structures of capital. Meanwhile, Black feminists such as Patricia Hill Collins came to emphasize intersectionality, collectivity, and difference as core parts of social formation. Intersectionality that is rooted in material and cultural analysis demonstrates the ever-present role of race, class, and gender. It is as true for the composition of white working-class masculinity as for Black femininity, each of which can be articulated in numerous ways. In this sense, white cis men are subject to gender, racialization, and class formation as is anyone else. And so the theoretical picture we get of class composition and class formation from intersectional theory is in one sense universal, rooted in the material relationships of property and exploitation, and simultaneously diverse and divergent, contingent on our experience with race, gender, sexuality, identity, and the like.

In the third and final section of the book (chapter 6, "Practice"), we move from a critique of capital and a theoretical grounding in class to the practice of intersectional class struggle in historical and contemporary movements for liberation. This tradition provides a power analysis that shows that we can shut down the entirety of the capitalist system through the withdrawal of our labor. As such, workplace struggles are an important site of power for working-class movements. Even for movements not directly tied to economic issues, the workplace holds the key to disrupt capital and win important gains. From here, struggles can be scaled up to political or general strikes, creating a situation of "dual power" in which workers develop mechanisms of self-management and workers' control. Many movements are already intersectional in this way, especially the Black Lives Matter movement, the immigrants' rights movement, the environmental movement, and the global feminist movement. An intersectional class analysis can help us better understand these movements and see new avenues toward victory.

The basic argument in *Intersectional Class Struggle* traces the evolution of class theory and practice for roughly the last two hundred years. We find that class emerges as a concept rooted in "material" factors, such as economic relationships, property, and production, but that very quickly the limitations of a strictly materialist framework to understand class became evident. New methods of thinking about class were needed. By the middle of the twentieth century, those in the class-struggle tradition showed that culture and consciousness played an equally important role, and that the two factors together, materiality and culture, had to be considered co-determinative. Theorists of race and gender then developed an expansive class analysis that could account for both the material factors of class, around economic struggle, and the cultural factors, around identity and difference. With some change, this is where the intersectional class-struggle tradition lives today and is the scope of the exploration of this book.

* * *

Coe is not the only person to identify a tradition of intersectional class struggle. Many before and after him have too. One was Douglas Fraser, a union executive and adviser to U.S. presidents. In 1978, as workers faced a new offensive from corporate boardrooms, Fraser wrote, "The leaders of the business community, with few exceptions, have chosen to wage a one-sided class war today in this country—a war against working people, the unemployed, the poor, the minorities, the very young and the very old, and even many in the middle class of our society." Fraser may as well have added women, immigrants, trans people, students, artists, the homeless, renters, patients, soldiers, and everyone else on the propertyless side of the class divide. The class war from the top is a war on all of us together—on the working class. These are ideas that Coe expressed in the epigraph presented earlier: we are "all in the same boat," we can "realize it," and we can organize and change things for the better.[15]

Fraser wrote his words in 1978 as he resigned his position on the President's Labor-Management Group because, he argued, the postwar accord between business and workers was in the process of being torn apart. No longer were workers given increases based on collective power and productivity. The new agenda, in the words of Fraser, was to "destroy us and ruin the lives of [working] people" with little respite. Fraser's resignation letter, now a historical footnote, marks the era in which we all live today. The turn of capital to neoliberalism in the 1970s has meant the steady immiseration of working people. This is not a metaphor, as segments of the working class are experiencing increased mortality. Following the 2008 housing crisis and subsequent financial collapse, half of Black wealth was wiped out. Women are 35 percent more likely to live in poverty, and wages for all workers are as low as they've been in half a century. Globally, workers are losing. These are the results of 40 years of Fraser's "one-sided class war" of business groups and politicians fighting very successfully to take back everything they can from working people. Yet, despite some recent resurgence, a meaningful discussion of class is remarkably absent from our politics.[16]

As Fraser rightly points out, in the United States and in much of the world, there has been a class war from the top, whereas working-class resistance has been slow against the onslaught. The class war is simultaneously a race war in the furtherance of white supremacy; a gendered war to support patriarchy, "traditional families," and binary understandings of gender and sexuality; a war against the environment; a war in the interests of state violence and increased militarism at home and abroad. Until we start thinking about the complex dynamics between these elements, on their own and in intersectional relationships, our ability to fight back against any one of them suffers. Just as much as the others, class, in its material and cultural constructions, is a fundamental component of the structures of exploitation and oppression in our society. Historically, it was the paramount concern of revolutionaries. That has changed. But sophisticated and vibrant class analysis that reflects the complicated nature of current class composition is necessary if any of our movements hope to win lasting change. In the interests of fundamental, emancipatory transformation of society, intersectional class analysis and class struggle are prerequisites.

Chapter 1

Experience

Introduction

"Like slaves." That's how Jessie de la Cruz remembers their time as an agricultural worker in California's San Joaquin Valley in the early part of the twentieth century. "The farmers treated the horses and the cows . . . better than the farmworkers," de la Cruz said. "At least they had shelter . . . but the farmworkers, we lived under the trees."[1]

Then, as now, agricultural workers faced difficult and dehumanizing conditions. Paid by the piece, the volume of crop they harvested, workers like de la Cruz moved at a frenzied pace to collect as much as possible. At a penny a pound, on a very good day, harvesting 200 pounds of cotton, a worker could hope to bring in $2.00. The piece-rate system "acted as a built-in speed-up mechanism" compelling workers to move faster and faster, despite cracked and bleeding hands, stooped backs with deep aches, blisters, sun stroke, dehydration, and other limits from one's body. It was no accident that Central Valley farms were known as "factories in the field." Farmworkers and their families, who often worked in the fields together, lived in labor camps that lacked "beds, ovens, toilets, showers and running water." Belén Flores remembered, "We suffered a lot, working in the camps."[2]

Luis Lima, another farmworker and labor organizer, framed their conditions as part of the system of capitalism: "All of the companies that were here in the San Joaquin Valley were strong companies that were protected by Wall Street. Only the people in charge here and the landowners—these were the ones who had the power. And so we got nothing . . . You were a voluntary slave. Around here, we meant nothing to the ranchers." "Voluntary slaves" or "like slaves"; the metaphor these workers used to define their own conditions, slavery, is commonly used by wage workers. Cotton has a long history with slavery, of course. It was the primary crop American slavery produced in the nineteenth century. But this was not nineteenth-century chattel slavery, this was something different, a new kind of labor, with new kinds of workers and new class relations. Capitalism and wages were producing new forms of exploitation, new classes, and new sites of struggle that were in some ways comparable to slavery.[3]

The voices of de la Cruz, Flores, and Lima reflect a collective experience, a class consciousness, that is both specific to their circumstances and transcends their particular moment in the history of working-class struggle. Myriad factors all shaped their understanding of the class-structured society in which they struggled for dignity, recognition, and a better life. These factors included experiences of exploitation, racism, and violence on the job; ethnicity, immigration status, and labor militancy; the impact of transnational companies; and their own personal experiences, ideas, and aspirations. This intersection—of material factors made from social structures and working conditions, and cultural or ideological factors made from experiences and identities—is the foundation of class. With other voices, their class analysis shares a critique of capitalist labor regimes as a form of slavery and in some instances it has been the foundation of an emancipatory movement, part of a larger project of human emancipation from exploitation and oppression.

This chapter and the next explore the insights and consciousness of workers themselves as they came to understand modern capitalism and class society. The very first industrial workers in Britain and the United States developed a penetrating anti-capitalist movement that placed waged exploitation and property ownership at the heart of their critique. In the American context, industrial work regimes resembled slavery in the loss of control of our labor, so much so that wage labor was debated as a form of slavery in the early abolitionist press. Wages carried a twofold curse similar to the American slave system: a careful accounting to maximize the exploitation of laborers, and racism and racial divisions designed to make class solidarities more difficult. In fact, as the theorist Cedric Robinson points out, tensions between English and Irish workers made race a crucial part of class formation in every context; he argues that race is always co-formed with class. From its very foundation then, capitalism created racial processes of class formation.

In addition to race, women's role as workers and members of the working class adds further complexity to the totality of class. Women were the first industrial labor force in the United States. Their double exploitation as women and workers led them to develop a form of class militancy, expressed in the identity of the "factory girl" that simultaneously challenged capitalism and patriarchy and created an early working-class feminism. Women excluded from the workforce were still part of the working class in the form of exploited "reproductive labor" that allowed profitable accumulation to continue; in fact, their unpaid labor greatly contributed to the profit-making process. They came to see capitalism and patriarchy as mutually reinforcing systems of control that needed to be struggled against holistically. Here capitalism and class emerge in the experiences and articulations of working-class women as co-formed with patriarchy and gender constructions.

It must be noted here, in these two chapters, that we analytically make distinctions between gender constructions of class versus ones based on race or property. But these divisions are abstractions meant to elucidate aspects of class and class formation for didactic purposes. Even though we start with English male workers, they are being "racialized" and gendered by the same material and cultural factors as are women, Black workers, and other workers of color. Therefore, racial formation for white male workers is just as much a phenomenon as it is for racialized "others," as we'll explore later in this book. Another factor we'll explore later is the concept of social "totality," that all these factors come together to make a complementary whole of capitalism, race, gender, and class, even though we separate them here for the purposes of explanation. This totality is reflected in people's lived experiences, in which they commonly make these connections on their own in their critique of the totality of capitalism. It is difficult, however, to express this totality in writing without abstracting so that we can more easily explore the component parts.

Given this diversity, all these workers faced very different circumstances and developed their own particular, intersectional varieties of class consciousness. But they also encountered similar systems—capital—that gave elements of their experiences a shared core experience—class—despite their differences. One part of that shared experience was the institution of the wage. Workers came to see wages as fundamentally antithetical to human freedom. Held within the wage was a "permanent antagonism," a conflict between workers' wages and employers' profits. At the root of this conflict was property. For employers who controlled property, its ownership did not come from a just division of work and responsibility but a relationship of power that kept workers from seeing the full return of their labor. Through wages and property, owners were able to extract profits, to the detriment of working people. This was a system somewhat like slavery in its compulsion of laborers who were not fully compensated for the wealth they created. As more people encountered capitalism and wages, the dissatisfaction with wages was developed into a systematic critique. It was not just wages and property that was injurious but the whole system of capitalism and its core supports in racism and patriarchy.

Permanent Antagonism

As working people encountered the new labor systems of capitalism in the late eighteenth and early nineteenth centuries, they began to piece together a broad and far-reaching critique of capital and class society. This was the generation that switched from artisanal and agrarian labor patterns to industrial ones in which people worked to the pace of a machine and were paid in wages for their labor, not for the products they produced at the end of the day. We can see these early critiques particularly in the English working class, the first people to go through this transition. For example, workers propagated the idea that all social wealth, including profits, came from labor. Describing the labor theory of value, workers argued that, if all wealth came from labor, then profits for bosses and wealth inequality were illegitimate, a form of social parasitism. They believed that, instead of labor commanding wealth, labor itself under capitalism was turned into a commodity and was sold for a wage that did not reflect the true value of the wealth workers created. In a rather sophisticated analysis, the workers argued that the crucial relationship in setting wages was the tension between profits and paychecks. This is what working-class radical William Sylvis called the "permanent antagonism," the fight in the heart of capitalism between workers and bosses for a bigger share of the value created through work. With this framework, others went on to place the source of this tension in the nature of property, arguing that the institutions of property and wages must be abolished together to create a more just society. By the middle of the nineteenth century, a basic vocabulary of socialism and class struggle had been established by workers themselves. These ideas express the core "class" component of the intersectional class-struggle tradition, and they were developed by workers out of their early experiences with capitalism.

For example, as England industrialized, one major critique from workers involved the growing inequality under the new wage systems. With slums and urban poverty in places such as London and Manchester, the contrast between extreme opulence and misery made it easy to realize that society was riven by class divisions. In one memorable encounter, a coal miner from Northumberland broke into the home where the boss of the mine lived, stole some beer, and left a note to the owner criticizing inequality. "I was at yor hoose last neet," he wrote, "and meyd myself very comfortable [sic]." He noticed that the boss was single, had neither family nor children, yet had a large home with a "greet lot" of rooms, and a cellar with plenty of wine and beer, of which the miner "got ma share on." In his broken English, the miner continued, "Noo I naw some at wor colliery that has three or fower lads and lasses, and they live in won room not half as gude as your cellar. I don't pretend to naw very much, but I naw there shudn't be that much difference [sic]." This kind of inequality, in which whole families lived in hovels not half as good as the cellars of the rich, for the miner was inexcusable.[4]

Critiques of inequality were just the beginning. Workers quickly developed a much more robust analysis of capitalism and the class system as industrialism progressed. The *Gorgon*, a British trade union newspaper, argued in 1819 for a "labor theory of value"—that it was labor that produced all social wealth. At the core of this idea was that the machinery, raw materials, and capital contributed by owners were worthless without the role of labor to put them together, make something new, and create new value. With the example of textile production, then England's preeminent industry, the *Gorgon* wrote that "the raw material does not constitute one-tenth of their value, the remaining nine-tenths being created by the labours of the weaver, spinner, dyer, smith, cutler, and fifty others." In this view, it was not the cost of raw materials or machines that made products valuable but their creation in the hands of workers into useful and novel items. If current value came from workers, then so too did past value, and capital itself was a creation of workers. Therefore, when a writer in the *Pioneer*, another working-class newspaper, asked, "What is capital?," the answer followed unhesitantly: "It is reserved labour!" If wealth was derived from labor, then all profit comes from workers.[5]

The *Gorgon* went a step further, arguing that under capitalism labor itself was a commodity. Moreover, labor was not just any commodity, it was the most important "product" in that it produced other wealth. The paper wrote that "labour is the superabundant product of this country, and the chief commodity we export." Labor was the "chief article of traffic," in that it built the wealth of the nation: "by trading in the blood and bones of the journeymen and labourers of England that our merchants have derived their riches, and the country its glory." In this accounting, labor is not only the source of all value; it is also the primary trade of the capitalists, as their exchange of labor for wages makes all profit possible. This notion is akin to later ideas attributed to Marx—that labor is a "special commodity," one sold like the others, but also one that makes all the others possible. This was a layered and rich understanding of emerging class divisions by workers themselves that included an analysis of inequality, the labor theory of value, and commodified labor.[6]

From here, working-class radicals began to explore a key mechanism of exploitation—the tension between wages and profits. In the *Trades Newspaper*, writer Thomas Hodgskin built on the labor theory of value, placing the relationship of the price of labor not between the supply and demand of workers, but between wages and profits, essentially demonstrating that waged work was a relationship of exploitation and power. He argued that if wages were to increase, the extra cost could be taken from profit, it didn't have to result in increased prices. In defense of unionization, what was called "combination" at the time, Hodgskin wrote that "the most successful and widest-spread possible combination to obtain an augmentation of wages would have no other injurious effect than to reduce the incomes of those who live on profit and interests, and who have no just claim but custom to any share of the national produce." For Hodgskin and others, there was a direct relationship between wages and profits: what wasn't returned to workers was syphoned to the top in the form of profits. Here worker and capitalist sat in a relationship of antagonism between those who produced wealth and those who took it.[7]

Hodgskin also developed a complex analysis of profit accumulation. He argued that capitalists functioned not to contribute to production and use, but as intermediaries, a parasitic function that increased the cost of production to both worker and consumer. "Betwixt him who makes instruments and him who uses them," Hodgskin writes, "in steps the capitalist, who neither makes nor uses them and appropriates to himself the produce of both." Consequently, worker and consumer were wronged. Furthermore, the capitalist separates these two "so widely from each other that neither can see whence that supply is drawn which each receives through the capitalist." This is an idea akin to Marx's "alienation," in which workers don't see the use or value made from their labor and are "alienated" from the very products that they make. It was class divisions, Hodgskin argues, that made this separation possible, and both wages and markets are sources of profitability for capitalists and alienation for workers.[8]

Not only did early industrial workers critique the systems of capitalism and wages, they also articulated a new language of class that had workers and owners fundamentally at odds. In the 1860s, Sylvis, the president of the Iron Molders Union in the United States and itinerant organizer, argued that, because of the conflict Hodgskin and others identified, there could be no reconciliation of classes. Sylvis took the critique of inequality and the tensions between wages and profits and argued that they were evidence of an emerging "permanent antagonism" between workers and capitalists. Addressing supporters of industrial capitalism, Sylvis asked, "If working men [sic] and capitalists are co-equal partners, why do they not share equally in the profits?" What he saw was that capitalists "roll in luxury and wealth, while labor is left to eke out a miserable existence in poverty and want." And Sylvis was indignant: "Are these the evidences of an identity of interests, of mutual relations, of equal partnership? No . . . on the contrary they are evidence of an antagonism . . . a never-ending conflict between the two classes, [in which] capital is in all cases the aggressor." For Sylvis and others, inequality indicated that capitalism was working for some but not for workers. The conflict between wages and profits was creating a system of class division that contained a "permanent antagonism" between workers and their employers right at its core.[9]

The U.K.-based James "Bronterre" O'Brien, an Irish immigrant and editor of the *Poor Man's Guardian*, contributed to this evolving class theory. Comparing workers and capitalists to "two fighting bulls," O'Brien wrote that "these two classes never had, and never will have, any community of interest." He elaborated that "it is the workman's interest to do as little work, and to get as much for it as possible. It is the middleman's [the capitalist's] interest to get as much work as he can out of the man, and to give as little for it. Here then, are their respective interests as directly opposed to each other as two fighting bulls." At the heart of this, according to O'Brien, was "property—this is the thing we must be at. Without a change in the institution of property, no improvement can take place." For O'Brien and others, property ownership was a relation of power; it allocated wealth to the top and excluded workers from control of the products of their labor and the wealth they created collectively. Because of this, what was needed was a "revolution of revolutions," what O'Brien calls "a complete subversion of the institutions by which wealth is distributed." Political revolutions that left property intact were insufficient; workers' collective interests pointed toward a social revolution that would end property ownership, wage exploitation, and the permanent antagonism between labor and capital.[10]

All this is to demonstrate that English working-class people were developing revolutionary working-class consciousness. An anonymous "member of the Builders Union" wrote in the pages of the *Pioneer* that the unions would "not only strike for less work, and more wages," but that the ultimate goal was to "ABOLISH WAGES, become their own masters, and work for each other." Abolishing wages, doing away with property, staging a "revolution of revolutions"—these are very far-sighted visions of transforming society. This revolutionary working-class consciousness was developing organically, by workers themselves, as they experienced and reflected on the new systems of class and capitalism.

This vision was not without its problems and complications, however. Early working-class critiques of capitalism were built on troubling racial and gendered visions of social order. English notions of dignified labor were based on racialized notions of Irish dependent labor and patriarchal notions of masculinity. There is also a troubling conception of national "glory" present in these writers' theories of laborers creating "national" wealth. These are ideas that later internationalists in the intersectional class-struggle tradition would critique. For the time being, however, we can see workers developing a robust, radical, and transformative analysis of capitalism and class struggle.[11]

In the appraisal of E. P. Thompson, the principal historian of the period, "the line was drawn" for early industrial workers. They developed a class consciousness of the most sophisticated type, all when "Marx was still in his teens." Workers built a consciousness and politics of "industrial syndicalism" or revolutionary syndicalism through which they created their own "socialist political economy." According to Thompson, workers did so "not blindly, but with intelligence and moral passion. They fought not the machine but the exploitive and oppressive relationships intrinsic to industrial capitalism." This was a question of collective interests and sets of interest in conflict with one another. Thompson wrote that although workers demonstrated a "consciousness of the identity of interests between working men of the most diverse occupations and levels of attainment," they also were conscious of "the identity of the interests of the working class, or 'productive classes,' as *against* those of other classes; and within this there was maturing the claim for an alternative *system*." Because these collective interests were in permanent antagonism, a new, more just, and less conflictual system was needed to replace it, one without property, wages, and exploitation. These ideas, developed by workers themselves, are at the foundation of the intersectional class-struggle tradition.[12]

Gender and Class—Capitalism and Patriarchy

American workers were coming to similar conclusions as those of their British counterparts but with different experiences and from different perspectives. Much like in England, wage labor and capitalism were condemned as incompatible with basic tenets of human freedom. In America in the 1820s, 1830s, and 1840s, the first industrialized wage workers were women, not men. The circumstances they faced illustrate the ways in which gender and patriarchy were part of working-class struggles. For example, women workers couldn't vote and were shamed for speaking in public if they wanted to address poor working conditions and the system of wages. These women workers made a complex, if imperfect, analogy of their condition to that of slavery. Their waged work was in addition to domestic work that all women were expected to perform. At home, they were subjected to unpaid "reproductive" labor, the work it takes to get workers cared for, into factories, and contributing to capitalist profit accumulation. In this instance, the struggle for emancipation from wages was also one for gender liberation against unpaid reproductive work. And so, at the origins of the industrial system, capitalism and patriarchy were fused.[13]

Sylvis's view that there existed a "permanent antagonism" between worker and capitalist was complicated by women workers at the textile factories of Lowell, Massachusetts, who existed at the intersection of class and patriarchy. American employers preferred hiring women because their labor was cheaper than men's and because employers thought women were easier to control. But what made women's labor cheaper than men's? To be made "cheap" meant first that markets were setting the price for human labor. Those prices are determined by both material constructions of the market through supply and demand, and cultural and ideological factors that devalue women. This meant that women workers in the United States came to many of the same conclusions about wage labor and capitalism as their British counterparts, but they also came to understand that capitalism was fused with patriarchy in shaping their value to society.

Let's explore the labor-market constructions that contributed to making women's labor "cheaper." Once labor was commodified through wages, market factors set the price, the wage, for any given set of workers. This meant that workers were selling their labor, a part of themselves, on markets for their pay. This was a radical transformation of the relationship of humans to their work. In the era before industrial capitalism, a worker would produce an object, and the object was sold at the end of the day. The way the worker made money was by selling the item they produced, not their labor for wages. With wages, this was reversed; their price for work was set by the market factors of supply and demand of laborers, not what they made. With lots of workers with few places to work, the market price for labor decreases. In the United States in the 1820s, men's labor was rare and expensive, but women, restricted by cultural and legal obstacles to full participation in society, had limited options. Women could work as domestic servants, teachers, and not many other paid positions. With few places they could engage in public society, New England farm girls and women could be an abundant supply of cheap labor for the new textile factories. That extra "supply" in a market—a supply of human persons—contributed to low wages, at least lower than men's.[14]

Low wages were also enforced through cultural attitudes about women's inferior status and restrictions to the "domestic sphere." As labor is sold on a market, all kinds of consumer presumptions and preferences go into making the product more or less valuable. In the case of selling human labor, cultural ideas, stereotypes, and assumptions affect the value at which people can sell their labor on the market. At the outset of the nineteenth century, ideas about women's social participation were heavily restricted; these ideas were later characterized by historians as the "cult of domesticity." The "separate spheres" or cult of domesticity ideology held that the proper and natural social role for women was in the home, concerned with children and domestic affairs. Ideal women were seen as weak, nurturing, and moral. This practice not only limited women's employment and economic independence but also was a strongly enforced cultural practice about what women should say or do in public. These kinds of cultural beliefs devalued women's labor at home and at work, as well as reduced their market value.[15]

Cultural beliefs about women's proper sphere were made material in both labor markets and the law. Legally, women fell under the rubric of "feme covert," the legal standard that restrained their independence in all public aspects of society. This meant that all women were legally covered by the rights of their husbands or whoever was the family patriarch. As a feme covert, women could not make contracts, sue in court, own property, make a will, serve on juries, vote, or run for office: "a woman had no recognized legal identity because the law assumed that her husband spoke and acted for her." On top of legal restrictions, cultural norms prescribed women's "natural" role as that as nurturer and mother, her "natural" sphere of work and influence in the home. These limitations restricted her social role and affected the market value of her labor. Women were seen as less valuable in society, and those cultural and legal constructions contributed to the low market price for their labor.[16]

Clearly, these legal and cultural restrictions had economic implications. For example, cultural restrictions that prevent women from working in professional settings limit the competitive labor market for male professionals, raising their wages. At the same time, cultural restrictions provide an oversupply of women workers in other jobs that lowers their market price. This is one of many examples of how material and cultural factors are fused in the creation of class.

Some of these factors of women's social disfranchisement were class-contingent, such as low wages and working conditions, but some transcended class, affecting all women, albeit in class-determined ways. For example, a married woman's wages, income, and estate were the property of her husband. Divorce was a rarity, and financial independence was possible only for the exceptional widow or single woman. The combination of women's legal and financial second-class citizenship meant that women, according to historian Nancy Cott, faced "subordination to men in marriage and society, profound disadvantage in education and in the economy, denial of access to official power in the churches that they populated, and virtual impotence in politics." Cott tells us that "women's public life generally was so minimal that if one addressed a mixed audience she was greeted with shock and hostility." These conditions remained essentially unchanged from the eighteenth through the middle of the nineteenth centuries. In the 1830s and 1840s, changes to the law were made mostly to benefit propertied men, who could transfer ownership to their wives and keep property away from creditors. Factors of gender and class were fused from the beginning, co-constitutive but with different impacts and experiences depending on one's social position.[17]

Working-class women related to these cultural constraints in interesting and often complex ways. As historian Gerda Lerner explains, middle-class notions of women's domesticity in which the home was a site of refinement and leisure were ill-suited to the realities of working-class women's lives. For one, many working-class women worked in paid labor, in the factories, as domestics, in piece work, in sex work, or in other fields. Even those for whom paid work was not an option still worked, as mothers, housekeepers, caretakers, et cetera. This unremunerated work is called "reproductive work" because, rather than the "productive" labor of the factory, it is the necessary labor to produce, or reproduce, the workers that the factory system needs. More than just childcare, this includes the cooking, cleaning, washing, emotional labor, and other activities required to get workers back to the jobs to face difficult and dehumanizing conditions. And so waged women faced a "double day"—working for pay in the factory and for no pay in the home.[18]

The working women of Lowell, therefore, faced a bind. As workers, they were exploited on the job. They worked 12–14 hours a day in unsafe and difficult conditions in which workers routinely lost fingers or hands. Furthermore, when profits declined, textile corporations would seek to make up the difference by working the machine operatives harder, cutting their pay, or both. In the "speed-up" and the "stretch-out," workers would be compelled to work at a faster and faster pace, or perhaps move from working one loom to two or four. At the same time, women's secondary social status constrained their response to company authority and presented an obstacle to achieving economic and political rights as workers. Unable to vote and facing social ostracism and ridicule if they even spoke in public, working-class women came to recognize and challenge the dual nature of their oppression.[19]

For this group of women, a sector of the white working class in the industrial North, they recognized that gender and class oppression reinforced one another. We can see this in their writing and actions, as well as in the identity they forged, the "factory girl." Countless letters to their newspaper, *Voice of Industry*, were signed by "A Factory Girl" and defended both workers and women's rights. In 1847, one workplace militant wrote, "I am heartily glad when anything is done to elevate that class to which it is my lot to belong. We are a band of sisters—we must have sympathy with each other's woes." The author links class solidarity to feminist notions of "sisterhood," indicating that, for working women, fighting for labor and women's rights were one and the same. The identity of the factory girl was built on the collective work habits of factory life and the shared female identity of New England that extended through social networks of "sisterhood." The lived experience of women workers reveals the intersection of gender and class, and their identity, the factory girl, a synthesis of those experiences.[20]

The constitution of the Factory Girls Association, written during a strike in 1836, provides a good example. Echoing the ideas of British workers' conceptions of collective interest, it said, in part, that working women faced similar conditions that necessitated a recognition of common cause and mutual support. "Conscious that our cause is a common one," they wrote, "and our conditions similar, we feel it our imperative duty to stand by each other through weal and woe; to administer to each other's wants, to prevent each other's back-sliding—to comfort each other in sickness, and advise each other in health, to incite each other to the love and attainment of those excellences, which can alone constitute the perfection of the female character."

In this text, the conscious recognition of their collective identity and collective interests was about their gender, their "femaleness." But it was also about class and collective interests. The petition went on to say that the strikers were "convinced that 'union is power,' and that . . . we (being the weaker), claim it to be our undeniable right, to associate and concentrate our power, that we may the more successfully repel their [the capitalists'] equally base and iniquitous aggression." Their "weaker" status, a combination of being women and workers, prompted their action and their own empowerment—the resolution was, after all, written by women on strike. If class and gender are co-determinative in working-class women's oppression, it is perhaps no surprise that this synthesis was articulated in their resistance too. The collective aspects of "woman" and "worker" synthesized in the "factory girl" to create a working-class consciousness of solidarity.[21]

The "factory girls" of Lowell therefore had to fight simultaneously against capitalism and patriarchy to protect their interests. For example, one worker was threatened with termination for organizing, "for employing her leisure hours in assisting in the organization of our 'Labor Reform Association.'" According to Sarah Bagley, a major figure in the labor movement, the worker was targeted both for organizing and for organizing as a woman. In a scathing editorial, Bagley virtually shouted: "What! Deprive us after working thirteen hours, the poor privilege of finding fault—of saying our lot is a hard one. Intentionally turn away a girl unjustly." Bagley promised to ruin the name of the overseer for the firing. Linking notions of class consciousness and what we could call intersectional analysis, Bagley continued: "Our name is legion though our oppression be great . . . We war with oppression in every form—with rank, save that which merit gives." The problem was both the power of companies and the restrictions placed on women. Bagley and other working women could clearly see the link between capitalist exploitation and patriarchal oppression.[22]

As historian Thomas Dublin points out, the issue behind working women's strikes and political action was not a wage reduction or a pecuniary demand but status and control. One petition written by workers on strike highlighted the increasing power of employers that was "becoming every day more grievous." The collective power of employers, they argued, was "entered into to destroy the independence of the operatives [workers], and place their labor within the control of the manufacturers" and led to "monopoly and wrong." The main problem was not so much low pay and bad conditions, as unpleasant as they were, but the loss of control and independence that the wage system entailed. Factory work done for wages, at someone else's control and for someone else's profit, was regarded as wage slavery. Instead, they argued, workers should control their own labor and the products that it created.[23]

This loss of control of labor was a major issue for the factory girls, and they used the analogy of slavery to understand the new labor regime under capitalism. In the pages of the *Lowell Offering*, a literary journal run by the factory girls, one aspiring poet refused to identify as a "slave":

Oh! Isn't it a pity, such a pretty girl as I—
Should be sent to the factory to pine away and die?
Oh! I cannot be a slave,

I will not be a slave,
For I'm so fond of liberty
That I cannot be a slave.

This work by a factory girl expresses idea commonly held among the "operatives": that wage labor was wage slavery, and that those who ran the mills ought to own them. There is a lot to critique in this conception too. The author seems to think that her "prettiness" and "fondness" for liberty make her unsuited for slavery, as if all other enslaved people did not also share those qualities. If we see these standards of beauty and liberty as white, there is also a process of racial formation happening here too that is co-determinative with class and gender. This demonstrates the intersectional nature of social power and struggle, and the necessity to abstract these forces to better understand them. If we focus on class, however, the poem nonetheless highlights that working women used slavery as a metaphor to understand their conditions.[24]

In another written piece, an operative who identified herself only as "Ellen" laid the basis for her claim identifying as a "slave" in the loss of control of her labor. The regimes of factory labor meant that one was working to the pace of the machine, a pace set by the company overseer. "I object to the constant hurry of everything," she wrote. She continued: "Up before day, at the clang of the bell—and out of the mill by the clang of the bell—into the mill, and at work, in obedience to that ding-dong of a bell—just as though we were living machines." Loss of control, living machines, slaves: these metaphors were powerful because they spoke to the real conditions that working women and all wage workers faced. With private ownership of the mill not shared by the workers, they were compelled at the behest of the new labor regimes and ownership class into a permanent antagonism.[25]

The picture that emerges is a working-class feminist politics that meant taking on wages as well as patriarchy. In the lived experience of the working women of Lowell, capitalism and patriarchy were fused, mutually co-constitutive systems of oppression that needed to be undone together. As workers, the factory girls levied radical critiques of the factory system, condemning wage labor as "wage slavery," and attempted to influence the production process through strikes and worker organization. Employer power in the workplace was enforced by gender exclusions in society more generally, and these were both simultaneously material and cultural constructions. The cheapness of women on the labor market came from their lack of social opportunities elsewhere, restrictions that were made in cultural conceptions of women's proper role in society. When women became the first industrial workforce and encountered wages for the first time, they leveled a blistering critique of the new system, comparing it to slavery for the loss of control of their labor and for the way in which they were sold on the market for wages. They also linked patriarchy to capitalism in their analysis and organizing. Wages and workers' control were women's issues, and patriarchal control of women was a problem for the working class. These were women at "war with oppression in every form" for a broader concept of individual and collective liberation.

Conclusion

In different times, and in different places, workers across the world have come to see wage labor as exploitation and a form of slavery. Twentieth-century migrant workers in California's Central Valley, early nineteenth-century British coal miners, and the "factory girls" of Lowell all created profound critiques of wages and capitalism. Besides the outrageousness of wealth inequality, capitalism robbed workers of the wealth they created by taking that value and giving it to capitalists. This meant that wages and profits were in direct contest with one another and that the class struggle was a permanent antagonism that could not be reconciled within the system of capitalism. Instead, a new system, one without wages and property, would be necessary to ensure that workers could control their labor and the wealth they created. For this loss of control, women workers in the textile factories of Lowell compared their condition to slavery and recognized that their experience was shaped both by corporate control and patriarchal control, which limited their autonomy and freedom. In the labor market, their statuses as women and workers were mutually reinforcing, contributing to their undervalued labor, exploitation, and oppression. In this picture, we see factors of culture, material conditions, and social structure fused in systems of class and gender that constitute one another.

But gender is not the only factor that constructs class; race does too. In the next chapter, we will explore the relationship between race and class and question how apt the metaphor of slavery is to explain the condition of wage workers. Although in some ways very different, many modern mechanisms of labor productivity under industrial capitalism were first used in the slave system. Slavery also bestows waged work with the legacy of white supremacy, in which racism is worked into the very structure of labor, markets, and identities.

Chapter 2

Slavery and Wages

As we saw in the introduction, when union organizer and Black worker Clarence Coe wielded that post to fight off white supremacists, he was simultaneously fighting against capitalism and white supremacy, and for worker empowerment on the job and Black liberation. Southern racists targeted him because he was Black and because he was trying to organize a union. For workers like Coe, the fight against capitalism and white supremacy were one and the same. This is, in part, because they share a similar root. The institution of slavery shaped the wage system that we now live and work under in profound and complicated ways. For one, slavery and wages are structurally similar in that they are both systems in which labor management and productivity are key parts of the profit accumulation process. For another, they are both systems of race in which white supremacy structures and defines the material and cultural conditions needed to make the system work, albeit in different ways. Indeed, the wage-labor system inherited these structures of exploitation and racism from slavery; modern capitalism was born from the wealth, labor exploitation, and racial constructions of the slave system.

But this does not mean that slavery and wages are identical. When workers say that they are "like slaves," the "like" in that comparison is important. This chapter explores the ways in which slavery and wages are alike and not, as well as the profound inheritance capitalism gained from slavery. It argues that class must be understood in its intersections with race and gender, and that the process of making class is a historical process that draws on the racist and exploitative labor regimes developed under slavery. Most obviously, the slave system and the wage system are both social relationships of labor exploitation. In both, workers lose control of their own labor, which is used for the profit of others. They are also systems of racial hierarchy in which Black labor occupies a lower tier on labor markets and in the social order. Indeed, white supremacy as a system developed to prevent interracial class solidarities from forming between white and Black workers by providing social and psychological benefits to whites, helping them to identify with white elites rather than Black workers. Institutionalized racial chattel slavery developed for these purposes, and its legacy continues into the present in segmented job markets, anti-Black violence, and racial hostility. Chapter 2 concludes by bringing together the elements of gender, race, and class to define the intersectional class-struggle tradition in the way workers themselves have articulated it. As the experience of workers like Coe and others testify, the wage system was and is exploitative, violent, and in limited ways comparable to slavery.

White Supremacy

The legacy of American slavery gave modern work a dual inheritance. First, the systems and methods of labor control and labor productivity are shared by wages and slavery, both of which pursue a frenzied dedication to extracting more profit per worker. The other is white supremacy, which has contributed to every aspect of class formation from the industrial period to this day.

Some tend to think of racial categories as fixed and immutable, as clear as black and white. But this is not the case; race, like class, has always been under constant strain and tension, is constantly being made and remade. Part of that remaking is contingent on class formation, on the particular interests and purposes of labor regimes and collective political desires. In this way, race, class, and gender are co-constitutive and historically contingent. From the origin of modern slavery to present-day wages, race was consciously used as a tool to divide workers from one another and to provide a variegated system of rewards and benefits to workers, some material, some cultural and social. It is important to note at the outset that racial dynamics take on their own logic and material constructions as they play out in history. They are not mere facets or components contained within the class struggle. Race, racism, and white supremacy are in many ways their own phenomena and, as many have rightly argued, predate modern class formation. Factors of race are just as present for white as they are for Black workers and other racial constructions. And they affect class and class struggle in important and complex ways. But race also contains components of class composition, and we can see evidence of the intersectional nature of race and class in wages and slavery, in the history of labor systems in the United States.[1]

Let's begin with the example of colonial Virginia. The story is complicated, but it demonstrates the possibility of interracial class solidarity for white and Black colonial workers, and the way white supremacy was used to break those solidarities. In seventeenth-century Virginia, Black and white workers faced similar social positions. This in part came from the equality of working conditions that both Black and white unfree laborers found themselves in. White workers were brought over as indentured servants, bonded workers like enslaved people for whom freedom was deferred for a time while they paid off a contract. During that time, indentured workers received no pay, worked in fields or as domestics, could be beaten, and routinely were subjected to violence. Enslaved Africans forcibly imported during this era faced similar work conditions. They were subject to similar dehumanizing treatment as white indentured workers but also had the possibility of freeing themselves and their families. And once beyond the term of the bond, freed Africans had some access to legal and social legitimacy.[2]

For example, the very first slave ship to the Virginia colony in 1619 brought 19 enslaved people to the tidewater region of Virginia. One of those, known only as "Antonio a Negro," later Anthony, obtained his freedom after working on a Virginia plantation. Anthony went on to own property and raise a family, purchasing a homestead farm of his own. Perhaps most surprising, Anthony was able to access the court system of Virginia, which he used in his favor. When fire destroyed some of his property, he petitioned the courts for tax exemption due to hardship and won a reprieve. From our perspective, it is remarkable that the white courts of colonial Virginia recognized a Black man at all. This is not to say that Anthony's experience in the American colonies was free from racism. But the racism and institution of slavery he found in America at this time was different; it was not the fully developed system of racialized chattel slavery that it would come to be later, and in some ways it was comparable to what white people working as indentured servants faced. Indeed, in the estimation of historian Edmund Morgan, all colonial workers shared a similar circumstance before racialized chattel slavery formed. "Servant, slave or free," he writes, "enjoyed rights that were later denied all Negroes."[3]

Enslaved and servant workers faced an equality of condition and social position that led to interracial class solidarities. Part of this was cultural. Like enslaved people, indentured servants experienced hostility and dehumanization from their social betters. Masters viewed enslaved and servant workers in roughly equal cultural terms. Both were "shiftless, irresponsible, unfaithful, ungrateful, dishonest; they got drunk whenever possible; they did not work hard enough or regularly enough." According to the ownership class, the English poor were "vicious, idle, dissolute"; they were prone to "Laziness, Drunkenness, Debauches, and almost every Kind of Vice." The poor were given to "mutinous and indecent Discourses" and were "Miserable, Diseased, Ignorant, Idle, Seditious and vicious." Arthur Young, a well-to-do farmer, tied poverty and idleness to labor productivity and industriousness. "Everyone but an idiot knows," he wrote, "that the lower classes must be kept poor, or they will never be industrious." In fact, such well-known social philosophers and society figures such as Bishop Berkeley and Francis Hutcheson favored enslaving beggars and "idle vagrants" and giving them to "manufacturing companies."[4]

These familiar attitudes directed toward enslaved and servant workers were based on similar social positions, similar class relations. Both white indentured servant and Black enslaved workers occupied a similar position in the class hierarchy of colonial society. They both were given difficult work in the field or home, both subject to violence to enforce productivity, and both provided the meanest conditions for survival and upkeep. Here is how Morgan characterizes Virginian planters' treatment of indentured servant workers: "[For enslaved and servant workers], the mode of operation was the same. The seventeenth-century plantation already had its separate quartering house or houses for the servants. Their labor was already supervised in groups of eight or ten by an overseer. They were already subject to 'correction' by the whip. They were already often underfed and underclothed. Their masters already lived in fear of their rebelling." Consequently, there were similarities of social status born of shared exploitation that shaped cultural attitudes regarding white and Black workers and made interracial class solidarities possible.[5]

In the period before 1660, then, similar conditions for white servant and enslaved Black workers produced class solidarities. Colonial workers, servant and enslaved, Black and white, worked alongside one another, lived with each other, developed relationships together, and had a shared community of interest in relation to the master class. "Black men and white," writes Morgan, "serving the same master worked, ate, and slept together and together shared in escapades, escapes and punishments." As a result, for servant and enslaved workers, "the two despised groups initially saw each other as sharing the same predicament. It was common, for example, for servants and slaves to run away together, steal hogs together, get drunk together," and to "make love together." These were class solidarities and collective interests that were fused in the shared experience of exploited labor in colonial Virginia. An interracial class solidarity was forming out of these shared conditions, experiences, and ideas. And again we see that these solidarities were at once cultural, material, social, and political.[6]

Colonial workers acted on their shared interests, often alone, sometimes in collective acts of resistance. The most famous, Bacon's Rebellion of 1676, highlights the possibility for interracial class alliances forged by those on the bottom of colonial society. The rebellion itself and the legacy it represents offers a complicated mix of race, class, colonialism, violence, and resistance. Initially, Nathaniel Bacon, for whom the uprising takes its name, wanted to expand the colonial frontier into lands of the Nanticoke and Doeg Indigenous peoples. This was an important claim for freed servant and enslaved people who found land inaccessible around the increasingly crowded Chesapeake. The colonial governor of the time, William Berkeley, refused.

A rebellion then formed around Bacon, composed of the colonial underclass both white and Black, who turned their ire on colonial elites. They marched on the capital city and burned it to the ground, forcing Governor Berkeley to flee to the protection of offshore British warships. Eventually, through deceit and violence, the rebellion was overcome. Bacon died of dysentery, and the last band of holdouts was an interracial group of Black and white rebels who were captured not long after.[7]

What is important for our purposes is that Black and white colonial workers who faced similar conditions united against the colonial ruling elite with enough energy to sack the seat of government. Needless to say, this was a serious threat to the interests of the ruling class. According to Morgan, elites needed a mechanism to prevent such powerful class solidarities from threatening their power again. "For those with eyes to see," Morgan writes, "there was an obvious lesson in the rebellion. Resentment of an alien race [Indigenous peoples] might be more powerful than resentment of an upper class. For men bent on the maximum exploitation of labor the implication should have been clear." The lessons of Bacon's Rebellion for the ruling elite were that racial hatred could be used politically to stem conflict rooted in the class system. After all, the rebels primarily wanted Indigenous lands, not necessarily to overthrow their masters. But there was another lesson, and this came from the threat of an interracial rebellion. Class solidarities between exploited Black and white workers had the power to topple their government and threaten the entirety of the colonial project. This was a serious threat to the ruling class. For many planters, "the answer to the problem," writes Morgan, "was racism, to separate dangerous free whites from dangerous slave blacks by a screen of racial contempt."[8]

It is at this point that racial hatred was institutionalized to create a system of material and cultural benefit for whites. This is the construction of the modern system of white supremacy; after this, racial attitudes of whites toward Blacks were fused in the governing systems of society. The master class that controlled colonial government began to establish laws to enforce segregation of enslaved Black people and white workers. A 1661 law, the first to recognize slavery, attempted to punish enslaved and servant workers who ran away together by adding years of service to the servant workers' indebtedness. The only way to punish enslaved workers, however, was to "inflict higher pain" or legislate away slaves' already very limited mobility. This is exactly what happened. A 1669 law, "an act about the casuall [sic] killing of slaves," decriminalized a master's or overseer's murder of an enslaved person. For runaway enslaved people or those in mutiny, it became "lawful for any person or persons whatsoever, to kill and destroy such slaves by such ways and means as he, she or they shall think fit, without accusation or impeachment of any crime for the same." For those enslaved people captured alive, the master was allowed to petition the court to torture "any such incorrigible slave" for the purposes of punishment and terrorism—to keep "others from the like practices." According to some laws, taxpayers would compensate slave owners for their lost property. The slave system was being constructed as more violent and more severe than other forms of unfree labor or involuntary servitude.[9]

Through law, the colonial legislature also deliberately racialized the difference between the condition of the servant and enslaved person. A 1680 law mandated severe punishment for an enslaved person or "any negro" who struck any white person. The law was "particularly effective . . . in that it allowed servants to bully slaves without fear of retaliation, thus placing them psychologically on par with masters." Additionally, masters were prevented by law from whipping naked white servants. Sexuality and sexual reproduction were also a clear focal point to enforce white supremacy. A 1662 law made the legal status of children dependent on the condition of their mother, allowing skin color and slave status to be drawn closer together. In 1691 and again in 1705, the House of Burgess passed anti-miscegenation laws, severely punishing white women who had racially mixed children but saying nothing about interracial children of slave masters born to enslaved women.

In this way, slavery was tied to the condition of Blackness. It was defined and institutionalized as a system of race. But these laws also gave poor whites the power to inflict violence as if they were masters, without carrying a legal penalty. Such laws went a long way to constructing interclass racial solidarities between white Virginians, rich and poor, and breaking the interracial class solidarities of rebellion and resistance.[10] All whites thus came to benefit from what W.E.B. Du Bois called a "psychological wage" of white supremacy, cultural and social benefits of race, while those whites on the bottom were still exploited for their labor. This form of white supremacy—shaped by class interests and at once material and cultural—had lasting impacts on Black and white workers.[11]

Lordship and Bondage

Although slavery was defined by race, at its core it is a system of labor exploitation. And, by the nineteenth century, the women of Lowell's factories from the previous chapter routinely used the metaphor of slavery to understand the new wage system. But is this comparison between wage workers of the North and the Southern slave system reasonable? The factory girls were making this comparison, remember, at a time when chattel slavery existed and was the basis for much of the American economy, if not the whole of American society in the antebellum period. On the single issue of the loss of control of one's body and one's labor (a definition at the heart of any form of slavery), if we listen to the voices and experiences of the factory girls, the comparison is apt. So apt, indeed, that the issue was vigorously debated in the anti-slavery press. On one side of the debate, if one focused on the loss of control of one's own labor, exploitation for the profit of another, or the dehumanizing aspects of being sold on the market (either in total or by the hour), the metaphor works. Where it doesn't work is in the direct ownership of human persons, the dehumanization of racism that supported that practice, and the application of violence to enforce productivity and control; these areas are where the wage systems had novel developments. For example, even though productivity standards could be applied in much the same way as slavery, discipline was enforced through a system of firings and blacklists that were distinct from slavery yet nonetheless show workers and owners engaged in a conflict over control. And although violence was used as an instrument of control in both systems, under wages it was made structural in the law and restricted to repress collective resistance by workers. As contemporary scholarship is starting to show, wages and capitalism inherited a lot from the slave system.

The similarities between wages and slavery were so striking that early industrial generations debated whether to include undoing wage labor as a goal of the American abolition movement against slavery. In the pages of the leading abolitionist newspaper, William Lloyd Garrison's *The Liberator*, a vigorous debate on the question of wages appeared in the early 1830s. Responding to the ideas initiated by the factory women of Lowell, Garrison himself rejected the comparison, writing that it was "criminal" to "enflame the minds of our working classes against the more opulent, and to persuade men [sic] that they are condemned and oppressed by a wealthy aristocracy." Garrison argued that, in democratic America, workers were not "objects of reproach" and that the concept of a permanent antagonism was "not true." He asked, "Where is the evidence that our wealthy citizens, as a body, are hostile to the interests of the laboring classes?" He found none, echoing contemporary arguments, because industrial commerce provides a rising standard of living for all. Instead, according to Garrison, envy was the cause of conflict around wages. "It is a miserable characteristic of human nature," he wrote, "to look with an envious eye upon those who are more fortunate in their pursuits, or more exalted in their station."[12]

Garrison, however, was confronted by leading figures of the workers' movement who pushed the issue. William West, a labor movement leader from Boston, asked tough questions of Garrison. If workers had equal opportunity and faced no hostility from the wealthy, why then were workers found "living in the poorest hovels or meanest dwellings—subsisting on the humblest fare?" Again, the issue of inequality was one element of critique that the wage abolitionists put forward. But another was productivity and exploitation. West asked, "Is it not obvious that the process[es] of mechanical and agricultural labor are altogether too low, when an idle libertine, who produces nothing, can command the proceeds of the labor all around him, and live at the cost which would support a hundred industrious working citizens and their useful families?" Here West points to inequality, evident for all to see, as a leading indicator that something was amiss in a capitalist society divided by class. And he also points to exploitation, the idea that workers produce for the profit of another, much like slavery, as a major point for the abolition of wages.[13]

West's strongest claim came in the direct comparison of slavery and wage labor, and he identified two key elements that make them comparable. One is a loss of control of one's own labor. In both waged work and slavery, a worker was held in a term of "bondage," whether for the term of their life or just the hours kept at work. Additionally, both were systems of exploitation in which the producer, the worker, did not receive the full account of the value of goods they produced. Both enslaved and waged laborers were deprived "of the fruit of their toil." In *The Liberator* debate, West addressed Garrison directly: "You are striving to excite the attention of your countrymen to the injustice of holding their fellow men in bondage and depriving them of the fruit of their toil." He wrote, "We are aiming at a similar object." On the issue of the loss of control of one's labor and work for the profit of another, West and others argued that wages should be included in the movement for abolition and human freedom. The factory girls of Lowell also recognized these similarities; it is no accident they named their lecture hall, which featured both abolitionist and labor speakers, "Anti-Slavery Hall." [14]

It is important to be clear about these comparisons. Whereas American slavery and American wage labor both shared the single element of the loss of control of one's labor, in virtually every other respect they were fundamentally different systems, with slavery being incomparably worse. Torture and violence were central pillars of the slave system, and violence was ever-present in the lives of enslaved people in ways that were not so for waged workers. Additionally, as slavery developed in the Americas, a hard racism grew with it. For people subject to slavery, this meant a constant process of dehumanization that extended far beyond their workplace, penetrating deep into psyches, leaving scars both visible and invisible. The legal structure and social relations of slavery were also fundamentally different than for that of wages. Enslaved people were owned in body, a level of personal violation and dehumanization that is hard to reckon with. As circumscribed as their options were in reality, workers could always quit, and refusal of orders did not always mean violence or death. American slavery was a category apart.

Nonetheless, control and exploitation of labor is at the heart of both these systems. In this respect, the critique coming from the women of Lowell and others makes considerable sense, as historians are now discovering. When analyzed as a system of labor, slavery and wages have a number of comparable similarities. Among these are the emphasis on detailed, individual productivity management and discipline for each worker, a system of rewards to encourage productivity, and the operation of the plantation economy as an "entrepreneurial" enterprise. In some respects, slavery was a system of profit accumulation and labor exploitation much like modern capitalism.[15]

As systems of labor exploitation for the profit of master classes, both slavery and wages focus intense scrutiny on the productivity of individual laborers. Large plantations had sophisticated labor management and accounting systems akin to modern business practices. Planters attempted to efficiently harness the labor-power of enslaved people and "blended information systems with violence—and the threat of sale—to refine labor processes." The result was to focus on individual productivity, with quotas, rates, and pacing set to maximize individual ability. Ongoing increases were scheduled to further squeeze as much labor as possible from each enslaved worker. Collectively, this meant an efficient system of production with growing rates of production and profitability every year. Slavery, much like capitalism, was a system of labor exploitation at its core.[16]

Techniques of labor management developed under slavery, such as the "pushing system," were later used in capitalist systems too. The increased production by enslaved workers was based on yearly productivity increases measured in their sweat and blood. In this system, year by year, the expectations of slave productivity were incrementally increased; a single enslaved person who was expected to cultivate five acres of cotton in 1800 was expected to cultivate ten acres in 1850. In South Carolina in 1801, the average harvest per picker, per day, was 28 pounds. In Mississippi in 1818, that average more than doubled to between 50–80 pounds a day. Just ten years later in Alabama, that number increased to 132 pounds per day. The result, in part, was a tremendous increase in the production of cotton, from 1.4 million pounds in 1800 to almost two billion pounds per annum just 60 years later. In aggregate for the antebellum period, yearly productivity increases for individual enslaved people averaged 2.1 percent, with a total nearly 400 percent productivity growth between 1800–1860. This rate roughly paralleled the increase in labor productivity of laborers in the North during the same period.[17]

One way that this system differed from capitalist exploitation was violence, as the pushing system was made possible by a combination of measurement and torture. At the end of a harvest day, enslaved people would have their daily totals recorded by the overseer and transferred to ledgers in the plantation house. After his first year of harvesting work, Israel Campbell, moving as fast as he could, picked no more than 90 pounds in a day. At that point, his owner increased his minimum to 100 pounds per day, under the threat of the lash, one strip for every pound short. Years later, when Israel had learned to meet his quota, it was increased again, and again. His final quota was 175 pounds a day. Another enslaved worker, John Brown, remembered, "As I picked so well at first, more was exacted of me, and if I flagged a minute the whip was applied liberally to keep me up to my mark." These labor management techniques combined with violence produced results; according to Brown, "by being driven in that way, I at last got to pick a hundred and sixty pounds a day."[18]

But planter entrepreneurs could reward was well as punish, and this basic labor-management strategy was also used in wage labor. For a job well done, or speedily done, planters would provide "fringe benefits"—extra time, extra food, autonomous garden or craft work—to reward their favored enslaved workers. Incentives went both ways: rewards for jobs completed and punishment for those left unfinished.[19]

The overall system resembled modern capitalism in its reliance on labor productivity and pursuit of profits. According to historian Edward Baptist, "Making more money allowed one to buy more slaves, thus harvesting more cotton, which meant yet more money." Planters calculated individual rates of production per enslaved person, identified as "hands," and graded them as "prime hands," "half-hands," et cetera. A visitor to Florida cotton plantations recorded, "A hand generally makes from 5 to 6 bales weighing 300 [pounds]—at 15 [cents per pound], five bales to the hand will give $300." In Yazoo, Mississippi, planter Clement Jameson calculated, "I shall make close to $250.00 to the hand." It was an old practice for slavers. Thomas Jefferson, paragon of Enlightenment rationalism, calculated the personal wealth he would accrue from each slave child born to his ownership who would work his smithery.[20]

The emerging literature from the new histories of slavery tell us that slavery was as much a labor system as a racial system, and an important antecedent for modern capitalism. One similarity was its system of labor management, which sought to control and exploit human labor to the maximum potential.

Labor Productivity and Control

For many workers employed today, subject to detailed time-management monitoring and productivity incentives, these measures might sound familiar. Slavery and wage labor share similar monitoring of worker productivity and extract as much profit as possible from human bodies. But they are different in important respects. Most importantly, under wages, productivity increases are not driven by torture. This lack of overt violence is crucially important. Without the threat of violence, waged workers had the ability to leave or to organize to improve their conditions, another crucial difference. But the wage system had other ways to enforce discipline: employers could monitor and dismiss. In the hands of employers, dismissals and firings took one of the advantages of the wage-labor system (the ability to leave a job) and used it to enforce labor discipline to the detriment of workers.

Modern capitalists, like slaveholders before, are obsessed with worker productivity. The most famous example of this is a system of labor management called "Taylorism" or "scientific management," named for its innovator, Frederick Winslow Taylor. To this day, most workplaces are governed by some kind of work-flow system that takes into account worker productivity. Taylor's idea was to maximize worker productivity, and profit for the employer, through detailed time-motion studies and work-flow patterns and routines. At the time, Taylor studied manual laborers to learn how to push their bodies to peak efficiency and exploitation. Today these efforts continue in time-motion studies, complete with global positioning system tracking and sophisticated monitoring systems, in companies such as FedEx and Amazon. There is growing literature that links the advent of industrial productivity systems to the techniques developed by slavers decades before. In the words of one scholar, "The administration of labor was carefully studied by the slave owners, whose achievements in this regard anticipated those of Taylor himself."[21]

Besides scientific management, there were other mechanisms of control. Under wages, the freedom to leave a job could be used as disciplinary measure against workers rather than contributing to worker empowerment. Firing an employee and industry blacklists were effective disciplinary measures. We can see this in early industrial work records that show employer attempts to arbitrarily control workers. Unable to use torture or coercive violence to discipline their workforce, northern employers used firings. When workers objected to employer control of their labor, or even arbitrary exercise of power, employers routinely dismissed workers.

In early nineteenth-century industrial work records, we can see a tense battle for control of labor in the workplace. For example, in the first ten months of production at the Hamilton Manufacturing Company in Lowell, there had already been 119 severances of employment, even though at the time the company only had 190 employees. Only 35% (42 of 119) gave "regular notice" of intent to leave. The rest gave improper or no notice or were fired. The reasons given for the loss of an employee were recorded by the overseer and reprinted in the company's end-of-term payroll account. They included things such as "misconduct, mutiny, disobedience, lying, captiousness." Only six of the discharges were for work-related performance, twelve were for family related issues, and the rest were for challenges to employer authority and control. Most of the discharges "seemed directed toward curbing defiance and encouraging deference toward authority in the mill." Such records indicate "a strong preoccupation [by employers] with the validation of newly-claimed authority through punitive controls." By determining who worked and under what conditions, employers sought to control workers more intensively.[22]

HAMILTON MANUFACTURING COMPANY DISCHARGE RECORDS[23]	
12 left without leave or notice	1 would not do her duty
13 left sick	6 went because their work was bad
3 left because some member of their family was sick	5 were discharged for lying misrepresentation, or circulation false stories
4 left to get married	1 was discharged for captiousness
3 left to go to school	1 ran away
6 were discharged for misconduct	2 were laid off for want of employment
5 were discharged for mutiny	1 was hurt in the machinery
3 were discharged for disobedience to orders	1 was hysterical and the overseer was fearful she would get caught in the gearing

1 for impudence to overseer	1 went because her husband came for her
1 gave notice and was immediately discharged for levity	1 went to work at the agent's house
1 gave notice and was discharged immediately	1 was discharged because her daughter was uneasy in the card room and made much trouble
1 was fired because the overseer did not like him	1 had written after her nam, emphatically, "regularly discharged forever"
1 was dissatisfied with her wages	

Importantly, the Hamilton dismissal records differ from the spectrum of opportunity available to southern enslaved people. Some of the factory girls were able to leave to attend to family, school, or other obligations—impossibilities for most enslaved people. But read in the context of workers and overseers engaged in a conflict over the control of labor, the "freedom" to leave could be turned into a disciplinary threat against workers. At least 16 of the discharges are for reasons having to do with challenging employer authority: mutiny, disobedience, captiousness, dissatisfaction with wages, et cetera. The two cases in which employees were fired immediately after giving notice show owners engaged in a contentious battle with employees over the basic terms of employment—whether an individual works or not. Seen in this light, those who left with no notice or "ran away" could have done so in reaction to arbitrary company control and to reassert their power over their own labor. For the employee, the stakes of the battle for control of the terms of employment were high; if fired, a worker was placed on the blacklist, thereby "regularly discharged forever." In terms of the fight over control of labor, the Hamilton discharge records could just as well have come from the Hamilton plantation of St. Simons, Georgia, as the Hamilton Manufacturing Company textile factory in Lowell.

As with enslaved people, individual acts of resistance occasionally found collective outlet. One of the five cases of mutiny listed in the Hamilton discharge records was for a work stoppage in the carding department of the factory. Caroline Damon tried to get the women in her room to join her in protesting low wages. She was targeted as the leader and fired, a tactic used repeatedly by the owners. In March

1830, Dorothy Wyman was discharged for having "combined to raise wages." Women were also targeted for not being proper women, as those fired for having a "bad character," being "not respectable," or a "devil in petticoats" could attest. The actions that stand behind these descriptions can only be guessed at. But they illustrate that company ideas of women's appropriate character and respectability included unquestioning acquiescence to employer power and control. Here capitalism and patriarchy are mutually reinforcing structures. And in this way, with employer or overseer unilateral control over the workplace, wages were and are akin to slavery. According to one historian, "The content of slave discipline reappeared in modern industry."[24]

The question of individual productivity and discipline could be enforced with violence in the slave system, but force could not be used similarly in the wage system. Nonetheless, violence became an important means of enforcing control around collective actions of resistance against wage workers too. As industrial capitalism developed, periodic revolts against wages and poverty created widespread economic disruption and threatened the social stability of the ownership class. As a result, owners became more adept at using violence to thwart collective rebellion. Most famously, this can be seen following the Great Railroad Strike of 1877, in which capitalists created a national system of municipal armories to impede any potential working-class revolt. It can also be seen in the creation of modern city police forces, which in places such as Chicago were formalized around widespread worker uprisings such as the Haymarket riots in 1886. In this incident, two workers were killed by police during a May strike in Chicago. The following day, unknown assassins threw a bomb at the police in retaliation, killing seven, for which the police and court system enacted their revenge by arresting, trying, and executing several labor movement radicals and union organizers.[25]

Violence therefore became part of the wage system in two important ways. In the first, violence was incorporated into the legal structure that virtually outlawed effective union action and created police forces to enforce those laws. The law also enforced exclusive property rights, a form of structural violence itself, a topic we will explore with the work of Proudhon in later chapters. At another level, extralegal violence could be used against strikers by police, private paramilitary, or vigilante forces in times of social protest or resistance. In the nineteenth century, as to this day, workers were killed taking collective action for better conditions. Although violence looked different between slavery and wages, it is unquestionably part of both systems.[26]

Slavery and wages were and are two fundamentally different systems, but at their core they are both systems of labor exploitation and control. When the factory girls of Lowell and wage workers in other circumstances called themselves "wage slaves," there is a lot to recommend their comparison. They were not beaten, did not face racial dehumanization, and were not owned in body as a form of property. But wage and enslaved workers both faced similar exploitative labor conditions. They did not control their labor or the products of their labor. They did not see the full value of their work returned to them but just a portion, sometimes only enough to keep them alive or not even that much. Both had overseers attempt to wrest as much productivity from them as possible. And whereas enslaved people were sold on a market in body, workers too sold their labor, their bodies and minds, for a time through wages. Finally, both were subject to forms of social violence, albeit of a very different character. Capitalist labor production therefore inherited from slavery systems of labor exploitation, management, and productivity.

Intersectional Class Struggle

What has emerged over this and the preceding chapter is how race, class, and gender are fused in the lived experiences of workers, and how those experiences are historically contingent. To take just one example, the racial divisions of colonial Virginia had a huge impact on the class solidarities of the San Joaquin Valley farmworkers introduced at the beginning of chapter 1. Whereas Mexican and Mexican-descendant field hands worked the farms in the early part of the twentieth century, in the 1930s during the Great Depression, scores of white migrants—"Okies," Oklahoma farmers fleeing environmental catastrophe and economic collapse—came to California looking for work. Despite facing hard conditions in the fields and various forms of cultural discrimination akin to racism, these workers were less likely to organize. In the words of historian Devra Weber, they identified their interests with the farm owners, as "many Anglo tenants and farm workers aspired to be property owners." As Weber concludes, "The migrants identified with white growers as Mexicans never had. Their desire for their own land and their concomitant identification with the white farming community joined them to their grower employers while racism divided them from other workers." This made organizing a class-based response to grower power all the more difficult. Here, in the farms of Depression-era California, the racial strategy of the colonial planter class bore fruit some three hundred years later.[27]

Consequently, we can see racial divisions constructed in colonial Virginia shaping the course of class relations from the seventeenth century until the present day. Throughout this long period, white workers have routinely sought to exclude Black workers from unions, job sites, and working-class communities. Asian, Latinx, Irish, and Eastern and Southern European workers were all subject to similar exclusions and violence. But Black workers bore the brunt of white supremacy. When New Deal legislation was enacted to help protect workers on the job and allow them to organize legally for the first time in U.S. history, both agricultural and domestic work were excluded as a way to prevent African Americans from these legal protections without the embarrassment of writing racial exclusions into the law. Now, 85 years after those laws were passed, new immigrants and other low-wage workers, particularly from Latin American and the Caribbean, face the repercussions of those exclusions. Contemporary labor markets are divided by a complicated network of tiered gendered and racialized access, in which whites tend to have access to the best jobs, agricultural work is relegated to immigrants in segmented labor markets, women are directed into specialized "pink-collar" fields, and the like. These labor-market prescriptions dramatically shape how one understands class. They are the modern fruit of these historical legacies.[28]

Further impacts can be seen in the nature of work and the experience of workers well into the twentieth and twenty-first centuries. For example, Black women working in Memphis in the 1930s and 1940s faced a double bind. Excluded from key industries and key jobs, they worked where they could. Often this meant service work, such as domestic or janitorial labor. When they were included in major industry, such as in Memphis's large Firestone and Goodyear tire factories, they were again given cleaning or service jobs. Black women had to fight to get anywhere, and in the postwar period this was through the union. Irene Branch, a Black Firestone tire worker in Memphis, recalled, "When I first went in, they'd give the hardest jobs they could to the blacks. They'd give you the jobs a white person didn't want. And you'd be making less money. It was really tough. You could be working side by side with a white person, and they'd get double the money that you got." This racial division against class solidarity is a continuation of the racial regime developed in colonial Virginia. For Branch, before the union, "the white women could get good jobs, but black women couldn't get in." But things started to change—"when we got the union," she remembers. Branch linked all these forms of oppression together under one system—"it's called racism," she said. But the mechanism to fight racism, and for liberation, was in class struggle. "The blacks just weren't treated right until they got that union," she remembered. "We didn't see freedom until we got that union in!"[29]

The experiences of Branch and many others point to the intersectional nature of labor exploitation and social oppression. They show that class and class struggle constitute a fundamental pillar of those structures. In practice, this often means that labor struggles are mechanisms to address and overcome structures of racism and white supremacy. For example, Lillian Roberts, the vice president at DC 37, a public-sector union in New York in the 1970s, saw unions as her civil rights movement. Roberts, a Black Chicagoan, grew up on welfare as a child and became a militant unionist while a hospital worker, winning election to shop steward and then going all the way to the leadership of her union. Roberts recalled, "The labor movement has [been] my civil rights movement." She found that labor acted like a civil rights organization because it brought "people together, centered around their labor, rather than around their pigmentation," an important mechanism to undoing systematic racism. But this was not a simple relationship. Black workers had to fight for empowerment in their unions. Black workers' first role, according to Roberts, was "to demand responsible leadership that reflects their needs 'cause it's very easy for labor leaders to become fat and forget." So the structure of unions had the possibility of fighting around race but only if made to do so by Black membership.[30]

The collision of the labor movement and the movement for Black liberation in the 1960s and 1970s had powerful impacts on workers.

In that period, unions were the "core equalizing institution" in American society. Once Black workers gained access to unions through civil rights struggles, they became a force for racial equity as well. According to historian Jake Rosenfeld, "By the 1970s African Americans had the highest unionization rates of any racial or ethnic group." The biggest gains for Black workers came from public-sector unions, and the economic benefits were real. Black women achieved rough income parity with white women in the public sector by the middle of the 1970s. Unions have their own sets of problems, and for most of their history they were racially exclusive, acting to uphold white supremacy rather than challenge it. Nonetheless, if made to do so by their membership, with a commitment to antiracism and intersectional class struggle, they can be and have been an important mechanism for racial liberation and class empowerment.[31]

Branch's and other workers' reflections here are striking. The economic exclusions she faced, as a Black worker and a woman, are summed up in a conceptual framework she called "racism." And, of course, she is correct. American white supremacy is a very real force, preventing her from economic opportunity and equality; white supremacy was and is part of the class structure. The solution, in her experience, was the union, a vehicle for class power; it made collective worker power possible and fought to integrate the workplace, winning real gains for Branch and women like her. This she saw as liberation, "freedom," in her words—a synthesis of class, race, and gender struggles embedded in institutions of the working class and achieved through collective power.

Conclusion

In all these accounts, class presents itself in all its complicated lived reality. It is not a static thing. It is not and cannot be defined universally for all people in all times. It is dependent on place, history, and people. Nonetheless, under modern capitalism, class has some clearly defined parameters that are virtually universal.

These collective experiences and reflections from English, New England, Californian, and southern workers provide the contemporary understanding of class. We learn from them that class is a basic division in society between those who own property and derive wealth and power from their property, and those who must work for wage. As we saw in the first chapter, the wage relationship—the social relations that allow some to own and force others to work—is a social relation of exploitation, akin to slavery. Contained within the wage is a relation of antagonism that pits bosses against workers in a ceaseless struggle to increase profits or wages. Waged workers lose control of their own labor, are compelled to work at the command and for the behest of the owners of property, and do not control the products and the profits of their labor. Wages also commodified labor. Whole persons were no longer sold on the market like enslaved or indentured-servant workers, but their labor was. Commodified labor meant that their value was set by market forces, a social relationship they thoroughly rejected. Furthermore, all wealth generation in society was predicated on labor. If workers were not the key beneficiaries of the wealth generation made possible through productive labor, then there was clearly something wrong with modern capitalism. The most far-sighted of the workers' movements saw a "permanent antagonism" in the making and called for the abolition of wages and property. The new order was one that they sought to undo through the construction of alternative systems of self-governance and workers' control.

American women workers built upon these insights. Their exploitability was made possible both through their membership in the working class and because their social oppression as women made them more vulnerable to the exploits of American capitalists. Their labor was "cheap" because of the restrictions of patriarchy that created a huge supply of women to work in the factories. But they were also cheap because, as women, they were seen as less valuable than men in society in general. For these workers, it was necessary to "war with oppression in every form," both workplace exploitation and gender oppression larger than a single factory. This synthesis can be seen in their writings and actions, born of class and gender solidarities.

The American working-class experience also exemplifies the synthesis of white supremacy and class exploitation, although it is by no means the only example of this. In the American context, both the system of wage labor and the "pushing system" of slavery emerged at roughly the same time. Both focused on maximizing worker productivity on the job through inducements and harsh punishments, much worse in the case of slavery. Both labor regimes benefited immensely from the American system of racism and white supremacy. According to the historian Edmund Morgan, white supremacy kept the American working class divided, making interracial class solidarities all the more difficult. It helped create a tiered labor market, one in which workers were relegated to certain confined paths based on race, immigration status, legal standing, gender, or other social hierarchies. Routinely, it meant that Black workers were given the worst and most difficult labor and held there through cultural norms, lack of economic opportunity and mobility, and state or extralegal violence. These factors came to reinforce one another, as racist notions of superiority and inferiority played out on the material field of class and property.

Therefore, we argue that the class divide is, in part, enforced and constructed by factors of race and gender. The structure of capital needs to create profit by exploiting unwaged labor, often that of women, which undermines women's social standing in other spheres. Similarly, racial capitalism enforces strict racial divides in the working class, forcing Black workers and workers of color into secondary job markets and segregated social positions, and rewarding white people with a "psychological wage," a position of social privilege that hinders class solidarity. And so too with queer workers, immigrant workers, the elderly or young, and on and on. These types of working experiences and social positions—based on wage, property, race, gender, and sexuality—are class; this diversity of experience in capitalism defines class.

For the San Joaquin Valley farmworkers, for the women of Lowell, for postwar Black workers like Branch, their circumstances were less than fully free. This was in part due to oppression such as racism and patriarchy. But it was as much defined by their collective class position—their relationship to the structure of society through property and labor. In their struggles to be free, we can learn quite a bit about our own moment and our own society. We are the inheritors of their struggles, both their victories and their failures; their lessons inform our own. The path to human liberation is with and through these legacies.

Chapter 3

Materialism

Whereas the previous two chapters explored the intersectional nature of the working-class experience, the next three look at the evolution of political theory about class. The theory of intersectionality uses the metaphor of "interlocking" or "intersecting" forms of oppression to help us understand how social power works in society. As noted in the introduction, the foundation of intersectional theory, albeit a significant breakthrough in movement theory, was weak when it came to articulating and understanding class. In this section, we attempt to correct for that shortcoming and argue that not only does thinking about class strengthen the usefulness of intersectionality, the methods developed in class theory, both materiality and culture, help us to have a richer understanding of race, gender, and other forms of social oppression too. With a material and cultural definition of class, we can supplement the weakest component of intersectionality and develop richer insights for intersectional theory itself. This section therefore is rather theoretical and develops a layered understanding of class starting with "materiality," moving on to culture in the next chapter, and finishes with intersectionality and Black feminist thought in the following one.

Materialism, as a tradition, has a literature going back at least two hundred years. In this literature, class is defined by one's relationship to labor and property—as Marx would say the "means of production"—which are important "material" aspects of class formation to this day. "Material" in this sense refers to tangible factors such as real property, economics, wages, labor, and, in some versions, social relationships. This type of analysis of political economy began in the liberal tradition, with the so-called father of Western liberalism, the English philosopher John Locke, who argued that what a person creates with their labor is rightfully their property. Very quickly, other Enlightenment thinkers and the emerging socialist movement began to critique this notion. They noticed that, outside of philosophy books, not everyone has access to property; in fact, those who do the work are not always rewarded by the benefits of their labor. Instead, property owners, through their mastery of the material world, could ensure that the value created by those who worked for them went not to the workers but to the owners. This split, around labor and ownership, in which property is a reflection of social power, is the foundation of class analysis and remains an important definition of class.[1]

From this, the early socialist movement developed a profound critique of property, class, and capitalism. By the mid–nineteenth century, Marx was able to synthesize the many diverse strands of the socialist movement into a unified theory of class. Known as "the materialist conception of history," or "historical materialism," this method provided many insights but also had many flaws. Its great strength was to emphasize the social structure and "totality" of capitalism and how that can affect consciousness, politics, and history. But it erred in that it weighted "material" factors too heavily. Almost immediately, anarchist thinkers and later twentieth-century Marxists such as E. P. Thompson and Stuart Hall began to critique the reductive materialist conception of class. They found that material factors were important, but so too were things such as culture and consciousness. This new understanding opened the door for a much more robust theory. Based on exploitation and the divide of property, class was mediated through the experiences, culture, ideologies, and consciousness of workers. Therefore, to understand class and capitalism, we need to understand both material and cultural factors.

In this chapter, we explore the material definitions of class that focus on political economy. We trace the changing definition of class initiated with the development of the "labor theory of value" by liberal thinkers in the seventeenth century. We then explore nineteenth-century anti-capitalist ideas produced by Pierre-Joseph Proudhon, who argued that private ownership was not based on use or production but power and exploitation, and therefore it could not be justified. Finally, we conclude with the Marxist foundation of class theory, looking at three ideas in particular: alienation, surplus value theory, and materialism. We argue that a grounding in materialism helps us think about the systems and structures that make class possible, and about where to best put our efforts for liberatory struggle.

Labor Theory of Value

There is a certain degree of irony in that the main idea used to justify capitalism, from its origins to today, also laid the foundation for the anti-capitalist critique in the nineteenth century. This is the idea known as the "labor theory of value"; and, as we saw in chapter 1, it says that all wealth created in society is only made possible through work. In its most consistent form, the labor theory of value suggests that the wealth, profit, and property that comes from work belongs to the workers themselves. On the basis that those who do the work should see the profit, the English philosopher John Locke argued that the labor theory of value justified capitalism and a government constructed to protect private property. This is a very common justification of capitalism to this day: work hard, and you will be rewarded. But later liberal philosophers saw some contradictions in Locke's theory. If applied with consistency, it would mean that the estate gardener and the hired laborer should truly own the estate rather than the absentee landlord. Once industrial capitalism came along, the wage system clearly violated the principle of the labor theory of value. Critics such as the French philosopher Alexis de Tocqueville argued that industrial capitalism also created a dangerous new aristocracy, an ownership class based on manufacturing capital. All this fell within liberal doctrine, and it was only later that anti-capitalist critics developed a more profound critique of property as exclusive and exploitative.

The labor theory of value initially arose as a justification for a new type of government, one based on protecting property rights rather

than monarchy, heredity, and aristocracy. At the fall of the feudal order, Locke was searching for a justification for governance not based
on divine right. He began to settle on the idea that government was
justified by the need to protect private property. But what justifies
private property? How do some people come to possess land or material exclusive from others? For Locke, the justification rests on labor. If one "owns" their own person, then the products they make
through their labor also become their own property. As he writes in
his *Two Treatises of Government*, "every man [*sic*] has a property in
his own person" and, if one "owns" their body, they also own their
labor and the things made through their labor. To use his example, a
person walking in a forest can harvest an apple and eat it as their own
because they took the work to remove it from nature. According to
Locke, the apple harvester "mixed" their labor with nature, whereby
facets of the natural world, once held in common by all, became the
private property of an individual. Even though this use is exclusive—
property takes away the apple from everyone else—it doesn't require
the consent of those who lost the apple because the owner makes
"industrious" use of it. What Locke means is that seizing resources
from the earth and thereby denying others use of those same resources need no other justification than the ability to take them and make
"improved" use of them.[2]

It is important to take note of the complex intersectionality of
ideas in Locke's work that act as a microcosm of intersectionality in
capitalism. Although Locke is focused on a causal chain of reasoning
between labor, property, and governance, he can't help but rely on
resource extraction and exploitation of Indigenous peoples and the
natural world. Indeed, in the aforementioned example, Locke identifies the apple picker as a "wild Indian," no doubt a racist construction
with the use of "wild" implying untamed, uncivilized, and not fully industrious. He also perpetually assumes male subjects, using the word
"man" not as a signifier of all of humanity but of men and not wom-
en. Consequently, in his work is a layered justification of property
that relies not only on labor but on racial and gendered constructions
of non-capitalist land use as lesser. Here then is a justification for European colonial dominance of the globe, as well as exploitation of nature to support capitalist property accumulation. Perhaps this should
not be a surprise because Locke was writing not only at the outset of

British capitalism but also British colonial conquest of the Americas, India, and other parts of the globe. What is important for us to note for now is that not only in the practice of capitalism, but also in its very ideological justifications, capitalism relies on multiple forms of exploitation and oppression, not only entailing labor and class but also race and gender. As Locke shows us here, this is also a question of colonial domination and resource extraction and exploitation as fundamental parts of the capitalist totality.[3]

What is more remarkable, and centrally important for our purposes regarding class, Locke justifies this resource extraction and private property even if the work is performed by dependent labor. If others labor for you, they are not entitled to that property, but the owners or the masters of that labor are. Locke reasons, "thus the grass my horse has bit; the turfs my servant has cut; and the ore I have digged . . . become my property." When Locke says "the turfs my servant has cut," he means that the field work and agricultural work done by servant workers accrue to the property owner, and not the laborer, as the labor theory of value would suggest. Although unspoken, we could add to his formulation the unpaid labor of women, servants, slaves, and other social dependents as outside the field of vision for Locke's justifications. This framing of dependent labor was not an oversight but a key purpose of Locke's work. Locke was arguing against the feudal order of aristocratic rule and in favor of emergent capitalist principles based on private property, enclosure, colonial conquest, exploitation, and, importantly, class divisions.[4]

Consequently, for Locke, government and the state are justified by the need to protect private property, and private property is justified through individual labor. Locke's work is a defense of class-riven society, one that is defined along the fulcrum of property ownership, with proprietors and laborers falling on either side of the class divide. For those with property, civil society and government were to be constructed for them, profits from others' labor were to accrue to them, resource extraction and colonial expansion was to benefit them, and government was constructed to serve their propertied class interests. Those doing the work, if dependent laborers, in Locke's view, had no similar benefits.

There were, however, a number of Enlightenment thinkers who disagreed with Locke's formulation. Writing in 1792, the German philosopher and educator Wilhelm von Humboldt took the labor theory of value and extended it to workers too, arguing that only work warrants property. Unlike Locke, for Humboldt, even in relations of dependence, labor justifies ownership. "The labourer who tends a garden," he wrote, "is perhaps in a truer sense its owner, than the listless voluptuary who enjoys its fruits." In this version, ownership is contingent on labor, not simply title or possession, a more consistent application of Locke's labor theory of value.[5]

Besides using the labor theory of value, Humboldt also placed the freedom to control and direct one's own labor as a core component of human experience. In this vision, labor is the foundation of human activity. As Humboldt argued, labor, rather than property, defines one's identity, as "man never regards what he possesses as so much his own, as what he does." Work and labor define who a person is, whereas possession is a transitory characteristic. Further, there is an inherent dignity in labor, as labor preformed under free will produces "artists" even in the most menial tasks. Labor freely entered is not drudgery, he writes, as those "who love their labour for its own sake, improve it by their own plastic genius and inventive skill, and thereby cultivate their intellect, ennoble their character, and exalt and refine their pleasures." Despite its onerous nature, labor under the right conditions could be ennobling, part of a process of personal liberation and self-discovery.[6]

Yet, for labor to play this role, according to Humboldt, "freedom is undoubtedly the indispensable condition." If labor is not freely undertaken, it is more akin to an "alien" imposition. In his words, "whatever does not spring from a man's free choice, or is only the result of instruction and guidance, does not enter into his very being, but remains alien to his true nature." Thus, if a worker is compelled to do work, "he does not perform it with truly human energies, but merely with mechanical exactness." Tasks and work imposed from outside one's control is "alien," not a part of one's free choice. Hence, a product may be made with "mechanical exactness," but the process has "degraded" the worker who has lost free choice. Therefore, for Humboldt, there were two aspects of labor to consider. The first was a more consistent vision of the labor theory of value, one in which laborers were the true owners of property. The other is that of control; when the laborer is compelled to work outside of free choice, that work becomes "alien" to the worker, not part of their identity with themselves but removed to a sphere of "mechanical exactness" without the "truly human energies," which come with freedom.[7]

Writing a few decades later in the nineteenth century, the French philosopher Tocqueville developed ideas similar to Humboldt. He found that the process of manufacturing, whereby a worker continually executes the same repetitive tasks, couldn't help but erode and degrade the worker. For him, in this system, whereby "the workman improves" his work, "the man is degraded" for the drudgery. In his memorable phrase, under wages and industrial manufacture, "the art advances, the artisan recedes." Much like Humboldt, Tocqueville saw that, in a wage system, laborers were alienated from themselves and dependent on employers. The worker "no longer belongs to himself," he wrote, but to his employment. This onerous quality of work is specific to capitalist labor relations and not inherent to human work activity, which, when freely undertaken, can be part of the rich and rewarding variety of human experience.[8]

According to Tocqueville, within a wage system, as value accrues to the top and workers decline, a new aristocratic structure emerges, with "some men who are very opulent, and a multitude who are wretchedly poor." In the new system, the employing class has no obligation to the laborers other than to extract labor and remunerate with wages. As he wrote, "The manufacturer asks nothing of the workman but his labor, the workman expects nothing of him but his wages." The resulting society is not harmonious but a system in which the workers are "generally dependent on the masters" and in which a manufacturer "first impoverishes and debases the men who serve it, and then abandons them to be supported by the charity of the public." Not only did wages and industrial ownership create class divisions akin to aristocracy, but also the very process itself alienated working people from a core part of themselves—their labor, a fundamental part of the human experience and freedom. For Humboldt, Tocqueville, and other liberal critics of wages, this was no model for a harmonious society.[9]

In addition, Tocqueville tells us the social relations of wages produce a class structure based on conflict and antagonism in which workers are fixed to a specific position in society. The manufacturing process "binds [the worker] to a craft, and frequently to a spot, which he cannot leave: it assigns to him a certain place in society be-yond which he cannot go." Hence, Tocqueville warned early on of the threat of the rise of classes in such a system and of the threat to de-mocracy. In his estimation, "The master and workman have then here no similarity, and their differences increase everyday. They are only connected as the two rings at the extremities of a long chain. Each does not leave: the one is continually closely, and necessarily depen-dent upon the other, and seems as much born to obey as that other is to command." This notion is strikingly similar to William Sylvis's "permanent antagonism," a new class structure rooted in conflicting interests of wages and profits. "What is this," Tocqueville asked, "but aristocracy?"[10]

The labor theory of value is a core component of liberal justifica-tions for capitalist democracies, but what exactly that meant was up for debate. All seemed to agree that, without labor, private property was not possible, for it was labor that created wealth. According to Locke and those in his tradition, value created by dependent workers was rightfully the master's property. For others, such as Humboldt and Tocqueville, this process was alienating, the rightful property owners were the workers themselves, and the new class divisions were a new form of aristocracy. What all these thinkers shared is an idea at the core of the liberal philosophy: a commitment to private ownership. This is the definition of liberalism, a belief in property rights as the foundation of government. As we will see, in the nine-teenth century, working-class philosophers began to break with the liberal defense of property and provide the intellectual foundation for socialist anti-capitalism.

The Emerging Socialist Idea

With the rise of capitalism and industrialism, we see the development of a political economy largely justified on Lockean rationale. Here a new generation of thinkers began to pick apart the Lockean worldview and the operation of capitalism. One of the earliest was Proudhon, the son of a French peasant and a journeyman brewer, a vocation he him-self worked at for a time before becoming an apprentice printer. His political education came through the turbulence of the 1830 French revolution, which saw the end of the Bourbon dynasty and the emergence of working-class politics in French revolutionary movements. Proudhon noted a class politics building up from the ground, from the poor and displaced artisans and peasants, and the small but growing industrial laborers who reaped little benefit from France's political revolutions. He rejected many of the core tenets of capitalism and argued that property was the source of much of the misery he witnessed.

By 1840, Proudhon had written his first major work, "What Is Property?" In this piece, he argues that property ownership is not universal but that there are those with and those without. Indeed, that is the very definition of property: to establish exclusive use rights that prevent others from accessing it, whether it be land, resources, machinery, knowledge, or other forms of capital. Refusing Locke's glib justification, Proudhon argues that exclusionary force is at the core definition of property, which means that it cannot possibly be a "right" in accord with other social rights such as liberty, equality, and security. Instead, Proudhon calls property a "negation" of rights and a negation of society because it pits the individual against the collective. "Property and society are utterly irreconcilable institutions," he writes. Further, the exclusionary nature of property, taking something away from others and absconding with it for personal use, is more akin to theft than any notion of "natural rights." He asks in his title, "What is property?" He answers, "It is robbery!" In Proudhon's estimation, property is theft.[11]

For Proudhon, property is not only exclusionary and theiving, it is also the source of modern class divisions. Proudhon, unlike Locke, did not assume "a state of nature" in which individuals were all equally free to access private property. Instead, he observed the world around him and noticed that some had access to property and others did not. This basic division meant that some had to work for a living, whereas others could use their property to make money. However, using property to make an income seemed morally dubious and philosophically baseless. The only possible justification for ownership was possession, a combination of "occupation and labor," and all other uses of property were illegitimate. If one used and worked land or material, they were justified in their possession; in his words, "the right to a thing is necessarily balanced by the possession of the thing." Like a theatergoer does not own their seat, nor a traveler the road, the notion of land ownership, of real property, was also faulty. Based on this understanding of transitory use and possession, private property as exclusive, permanent ownership could not be justified.[12]

Further, property is illegitimate in relation to profit from rents as well. Proudhon used the labor theory of value to argue that the wealth creation from property comes from the laborer who applies her work, not from the proprietor who merely owns. Proudhon argues, "If labor is the sole basis of property, I cease to be proprietor of my field as soon as I receive rent for it from another." As he argues, true ownership comes from possession. Rent then, in all its forms, such as tenancy and wages, is spurious. The laborer or resident is the true owner; once another uses their labor on that property or occupies it, they become the rightful possessor. According to this notion, property and rents are reflections of class divisions of power, not any legitimate claim to profit from legal ownership. Based on the labor theory of value, those who work for others, such as Locke's turf cutter, were more justified in the ownership of property they produced than the legal "proprietor."[13]

Proudhon's class analysis was founded on an understanding of modern capitalist production, class divisions, wages, and profits. He argues that wages necessarily did not pay the full account of value created from labor, but the profit taken from workers claimed through property ownership instead represented a form of rent not tied to labor or use. According to Proudhon, "The laborer retains, even after he has received his wages, a natural right of property in the thing which he has produced." And he emphasizes that labor does not solely justify simple remuneration, through wages or salary, but also ownership. A worker is the real proprietor, not "simply proprietor of his allowance, his salary, his wages, I mean proprietor of the value which he creates, and by which the master alone profits." According to this formulation, and much in accord with the labor theory of value, wages are illegitimate. The wage, he writes, "is not sufficient: the labor of the workers has created a value; now this value is their property." This would mean that profits accruing to a capitalist are also illegitimate. Merely owning capital or property does not justify extracting profits from its productive use by others.[14]

Whereas Proudhon used these ideas to argue for collective ownership, others, such as Peter Kropotkin, a naturalist, anarchist philosopher, and Russian prince, found all property illegitimate on the basis of the collective, socialized nature of modern work. Kropotkin's family put him close to the tsar in his youth, but he rejected this path for himself, choosing instead the pursuit of natural sciences, which led him to the study of anarchism and eventually into exile as an anarchist revolutionary. Kropotkin asked how, in socialized production, one could justify individual property ownership. If we consider a workshop with 10 or 100 people laboring to make a product, such as textiles, do each of those workers "own" 1/10th or 1/100th of each yard of fabric? How is property to be disbursed on this basis? His basic idea was that, under modern production methods, there are not individual craft workers who construct a complete product but hundreds and sometimes thousands of people working in small steps to create a finished good. In this matrix of collective work and social production, any notion of individual ownership would be absurd.

According to Kropotkin, even collective ownership, in which all the workers retained a portion of a claim on the finished product, would be untenable. To offer a contemporary example, a worker-owned computer manufacturer is not acting alone but in concert with a whole industry that is supplying parts, computer chips, plastic casing, screens, processors, mice, and other components. Do each of those workers also not have a right to ownership of the final product? What is more, Kropotkin argued that all these people were working in a historical moment produced by the labor of generations of workers past. They made the roads and the buildings, the telecommunications infrastructure, and the networks of shipping and trade that made present work possible. Surely those workers too were justified in a share of the final product.

Based on the labor theory of value, all this is true. But the labor theory of value applied in a system in which work and production had already been highly socialized no longer made sense. Kropotkin's conclusion then was that individual ownership is not just faulty but also fictitious. There is no way to determine who owns what in a society where all work and production are so thoroughly interconnected and socialized. Instead, Kropotkin gave us the best dictum of full communism: "All for all"—property cannot be justified and instead should be shared without distinction. If private property is bunk, then egalitarian collective use and distribution is the only just social model.[15]

In this, Kropotkin elaborated ideas already sketched out by Proudhon. For every individual, said Proudhon, "There is not a man, then, but lives upon the products of several thousand different industries, not a laborer but receives from society at large the things which he consumes." This basic interconnectedness means that "all capital" is only possible as "the result of collective labor [and] is, in consequence, collective property." Both Proudhon and Kropotkin came to an important understanding: humans are inherently social, communal creatures. In our regimes of labor, we necessarily rely on the natural world and the collective efforts of others. Private ownership as exclusive and individualist therefore is faulty, and the source of capital is nothing but the inheritance of collective labor from past workers. For Proudhon, property is social and collective and therefore should be socialized and collectivized. For Kropotkin, building on these ideas, the whole notion of property ownership is wrong and human production and relation to the natural world should be held in common.[16]

In the work of Proudhon, Kropotkin, and other early socialists, class is defined by the relationship of an individual to their access to property. For those with property, the things they owned can be used to control and garnish further wealth. For those without, they have to sell or rent themselves in a form of dependency and have the value of the product of their labor taken by the owners of property. The class division placed a central antagonism between wages and profits, between workers and owners, in the heart of modern society. Whereas proprietors wanted more and sought to achieve this by lowering wages, workers too wanted and deserved more and could achieve it only by forcing owners to give up profits. This is the basis of class politics, the foundation of contemporary anti-capitalist struggles, and a set of ideas that are important today.

Marx's Foundation

This work in the 1840s leads us to the figure most closely associated with class and class analysis: Karl Marx. Born in the western German town of Trier to an attorney and middle-class homemaker, Marx became a leading philosopher and activist of the communist movement.

Despite his accomplishments as a thinker, toward the end of his career, he posed a question that he was not able to answer. "What constitutes a class?" he asks in the final volume of his masterwork, *Capital*, an unfinished work published posthumously. Marx was attempting to establish a theoretical definition for class, one that could guide his work and provide a useful framework for political action. After a few sentences of speculative writing, however, the manuscript breaks off, and we are left without a satisfactory answer. Not having a theory of class is a striking omission in the work of Marx, a systematic thinker who placed class at the center of his analysis and believed, after all, that "the history of all hitherto existing society is the history of class struggles." His failure to articulate a definition of class is important because it reminds us not only that specifying class is a difficult process, but also that Marx was at times an incomplete thinker. His work contains important insights, notably on alienation, materialism, and aspects of "surplus value" theory. But these same ideas, especially an overdrawn materialism, also contain setbacks for constructive thinking about class.[17]

To be clear, Marx is an important thinker with unparalleled contributions to the intersectional class-struggle tradition. Not the least of which, his "historical materialism," is one half of any definition of "class" or "working class," as we argue here. Although Marx's contributions to socialism and anti-capitalist thinking are important, he tends to play an outsized role in contemporary discussions of class. Anti-capitalist analysis emerged from a broad social movement, largely from workers themselves, and assembled many of the basics of contemporary class analysis. These include the critique of wages, private property, and profit, social alienation from work, and the two-class model of workers and owners. What Marx did was take many of these elements and develop them, providing a systematic framework for thinking about capitalism and class. In some instances, this led to highly productive ideas; in others it led to theoretical dead ends.

The following section of the chapter will explore three of Marx's primary contributions to anti-capitalist class thought: the notion of alienated labor, materialism, and surplus value theory. We've chosen just three because they most directly address class and Marx's final unanswered question, but also because these ideas went on to define much of the debate about class into the twentieth century and beyond. Parts of these ideas became major theoretical problems for thinkers and activists of later eras. The point here is that Marx, like any thinking person, was complex. His ideas changed. Some were very useful and help explain our world today; and some were overdrawn or led to problems not foreseen when they were initially developed. It is important that we learn from this mixed bag if we hope to better understand and change the world.

Alienation

A key moment in Marx's political development came in 1844 when he wrote what many consider the early foundation of his later work, the "Economic and Philosophic Manuscripts." Not published until the twentieth century, the manuscripts show a class analysis in which Marx was beginning to take on the question of individual wages and property, and to think systematically about those relationships. In a class-divided society, with two classes, "the property-*owners* and the propertyless *workers*," the process of laboring creates more than the thing produced; it also creates social relationships. These social relationships of property are at the foundations of class, and through them the worker is also made into a commodity. Echoing ideas from classical liberalism, Marx writes that, with waged labor and industrial production, greater wealth was possible, but that "the *increasing value* of the world of things proceeds in direct proportion [to] the *devaluation* of the world of men." Wages degrade workers, but they also do something more; they create the social relations of production, the relationship of individuals to their work and to one another through class. The importance of this insight is that the wage relationship is not just individual, between worker and boss, but a collective, social relationship—a class relationship with extensive implications for society. According to Marx, class is determined by one's relationship to others, to social structures such as property, and is collective in that it is shared by those similarly positioned in the social hierarchy of capital.[18]

For Marx, alienation and labor were linked in a complex process that related to nearly every aspect of one's life. Starting with the workers' alienation from the product they produced, this relationship of alienation extends through to alienate the worker from other workers, from nature, from owners and other classes, and the worker from herself. At base, this alienation reflects iniquitous property relations, in which the product of labor is not owned by workers themselves. In waged production, the worker sees "the *product of his labour* as to an *alien* object," and the final product of work "confronts" the worker as "a *power independent* of the producer." Marx is trying to say that, without control or ownership of the final product of labor, workers lose the ability to invest themselves in their work. The more they put in, the more is taken from them in the final product, as the object is not their own. So, in waged relations of production, the worker is alienated from the product of their work. But this means that workers are also alienated from their very work, from the very physicalness of their productivity, as the harder they work, they less they get.[19]

Marx takes this critique a step further, reframing his notion of "alienation" from a moral critique of waged labor to a critique of the system of capitalism. Marx says that alienation is at once the product and the cause of private property. It is unclear exactly what he means in this respect. What we can say, however, is that wages, private property, and alienation reinforce one another. They are part of the same system, a capitalist totality that is about much more than just profits and property. As Marx says, "*wages* and *private property* are identical"; you cannot have one without the other. Thus, the solution to alienation is not to modify or improve wages but to end the entire structure of wages and property on which alienation is based. Whereas the "forcing up of wages" for all workers would only mean "better payment for the slave," the equalization of all wages, or the self-payment of wages as in worker collectives, would mean only self-exploitation, or one in which "society is then conceived as an abstract capitalist," as in the case of equalization. Therefore, wages and property, as two reinforcing components of capitalism, must be entirely done away with. One cannot "clamour for *freedom* on the basis of the slave system," Marx wrote elsewhere.[20]

In his more utopian moments, Marx thought that this liberation from wages and property could be the basis for "universal human emancipation." Ending wages would contribute to much broader forms of human emancipation "because the whole of human servitude is involved in the relation of the worker to production," and, for Marx, "every relation of servitude is but a modification and consequence of this relation." According to this thinking, labor exploitation in wages is a form of servitude that undergirds many others, and undoing this social relation will enable emancipation on many other fronts. Clearly Marx saw wage exploitation as intersecting with other forms of social oppression. Although the idea that every form of oppression or "servitude" comes directly from wages is faulty, we can take two useful ideas from this discussion of alienation. The first is Marx's systematic thinking of capitalism as a "totalizing" system, in which the entire structure of the system that produces alienation, wages, and property must be undone. The second is that undoing these structures contributes to broader liberation, a necessary part of "universal human emancipation."[21]

Surplus Value

Marx's concept of alienation helps us understand why so much of contemporary waged labor feels so bad, why the very process of working every day, the daily grind, is so dehumanizing. Yet this was an elaboration of notions of labor estrangement from other thinkers, one present in liberal political philosophy too. Marx and many other Marxists consider his main contribution to be his "theory of surplus value," the idea that labor is the only source of value creation in society and that wages do not, indeed cannot, reflect all this value creation if employers are to gain a profit. This is an extremely rich yet extremely flawed insight. On the one hand, the theory of surplus value can help us see the inner workings of exploitation as it happens in the workplace, in that the speedup, the longer work day, and labor-monitoring systems are all mechanisms of intensified exploitation. On the other hand, Marx most likely overreached in its application, attempting to show how all profit under capitalism comes predominantly from this relation of surplus value and how this level of exploitation explains not only profit but prices too. In both of these applications, Marx is likely limited in his vision. But that doesn't hinder the utility of the theory of surplus value to further our understanding of labor exploitation and class formation.[22]

A key insight in the theory of surplus value is Marx's emphasis that workers sell not only their labor, their time, and physical and mental selves but also their "labor-power," their capacity and ability to work and to work harder. Like others in the workers' movement, Marx noted that there is a difference between what the worker sells and what the employer buys. For Marx, labor-power is defined as the capacity to work. Crucially, this capacity has varying degrees of intensity—a worker can work fast or slow. By emphasizing that workers sell their labor-power, Marx could show that the level of exploitation in a workplace could vary in intensity as well. With speedups, short-staffing, lengthening the workday, or other gimmicks, employers could squeeze more value out of their workers while on the clock. This in part explains why so much effort goes into workplace productivity, efficiency, and time management.[23]

But labor-power is just one part of surplus value. Although labor-power is a commodity to be sold under capitalism, its price, the wage that workers get paid, is complicated. A key concept here is what Marx called "social reproduction." He argued that the price paid for labor, a worker's wage, was not determined like the price of other commodities under capitalism. The cost of the worker was a reflection of the cost it took to make that worker available—her breakfast, her rent, et cetera; in short, the cost of wages reflects the food, clothes, shelter, and everything else necessary to produce that worker in aggregate. This could include the cost of education or training if the worker is particularly skilled or other necessities to make their labor-power possible. In surplus value theory, wages are a reflection of the cost of the worker to keep herself going and maybe make more workers to replace her. This is the cost that employers pay in the form of the wage.[24]

According to Marx, whereas employers are paying workers the cost of their reproduction through wages, what they get is workers' labor-power, their capacity to create value through production. This is the core idea of surplus value. Whereas workers' wages are limited by the cost of their upkeep, the value that workers create through their labor is far more than their cost. This extra value, the surplus value, is taken by employers as profit. For example, if a worker at Subway sandwich shop gets paid the federal minimum wage of $7.25 an hour for a shift of eight hours, their cost to the employer is $58.00

for the day.[25] If the average Subway sandwich costs $6, the store will have to sell just under ten sandwiches to cover the cost of that worker and anything more goes to the boss as profit.[26] If the worker makes and sells ten sandwiches by lunch, anything sold in the afternoon is profit; or, if the worker makes and sells two sandwiches an hour, 80% of the price of the second sandwich is profit. However one looks at it, the employer is gaining value, profit, from the labor of the worker. The worker is not seeing the full return of their value. This notion of surplus value is a unique and productive contribution to the earlier labor theory of value as developed by liberal thinkers.[27]

The theory of surplus value as explained here allows us to see the interworking of capitalist exploitation of labor and workers. For one, it defines profit as the skimming of surplus value from workers. This puts labor and profits in inverse relationship. All things being equal, if an employer wants to increase their profit with the same resources, they will have to take it out of the workers' wages or labor-power. This could be done by reducing their wages, increasing the workers' rate of work, or by other contrivance. Similarly, if a worker wants to increase their wages, it must come out of the boss's profits. This is the central antagonism at the heart of capitalism. It points to the idea that, so long as wages and wage exploitation exists, there will never be labor peace, as each side will continuously be in contestation for advantage. "Upon this relation," Marx writes, "between the employing capitalist and the waged labourer the whole wages system and the whole present system of production hinge." This is unquestionably a moral critique for Marx, and more than just about property relations, a full denunciation of the economic system of capitalism. As capitalism is designed to create and grow profits, if all profit accumulation is based on exploitation and antagonism, then this is hardly a system conducive to human liberty.[28]

Surplus value is an important insight into the exploitation at the heart of capitalism. But Marx likely overstretched in his analysis of the centrality of surplus value. Marx's attempt was to show that virtually all profit under capitalism comes from this direct form of exploitation of workers. He mentions other types, what he calls "primitive accumulation," seizing natural resources through force or law, rents and interest, speculations, et cetera. But they are all secondary, according to Marx, to the primary mode of production of the era, industrial production with wages. Although the attempt is laudatory, Marx was likely wrong. Profits accrue through numerous avenues still, such as speculation, rent, and seizing natural resources. These are in fact important forms of profit-making to the present day. Additionally, Marx attempts to show that the price of all commodities is determined by the "socially necessary labor" needed to produce them, a formulation impossible to quantify, much less prove. But these shortcomings do not detract from the usefulness of the theory of surplus value in explaining the conditions of labor that we face and the relations of class under capitalism. Indeed, Marx's notion of surplus value and its relation to exploitation and antagonism is invaluable.[29]

Materialism

The third major insight from Marx is what has come to be called "materialism" or the "materialist conception of history." It is just as valuable, and just as troubled, as the others. Marx introduced ideas that material conditions—the economy, means of production, labor, class, etc.—are the foundation of what explains current social and political formations, as well as the leading factor that determines the course of history. According to this notion, the "economic structure of society" is the "real foundation" on which the ideas, ideology, culture, consciousness, and politics emerge and are dependent. Marx is suggesting that the methods of producing the material sustenance of any society, what he calls the "material forces of production" (farming, tractors, iron mills, and the like), give rise to various forms of labor and production and are embedded in human relationships, what he calls the "social relations of production." This could be ancient slavery, feudal serfs, or capitalist wage work. All this, both the material forces and the social relations of production, creates the economic foundation of a society, "the base," upon which social, political, and intellectual factors what Marx called the "superstructure" are overlaid in a conditional relationship. When conflict arises in society, it stems from contradictions in the economic base, particularly between the material forces and the social relations, which then leads to new sets of politics and consciousness. Ultimately, for Marx, consciousness comes from the materiality of life, and not the other way around. "It is not the consciousness of men that determines their existence," Marx writes, "but their social existence that determines their consciousness."[30]

Marx's materialism then is closely tied to his idea of "base/superstructure" as a model for social causality. Again, there is a lot to recommend this view. For one, it contributes to notions of social structure, ideas vital for understanding of society. In this view, "material conditions" (e.g., the ability to produce food) and "social relations" (e.g., class structures) form part of a hard "materialist" basis of society. Class relations "structure" how all of us see and experience the world; they shape our opportunities and worldview, guiding and selecting for certain outcomes and foreclosing others. In this sense, material conditions do indeed shape consciousness and culture. These conditions are material, they can observed and known, and they can be struggled against and unmade.

But Marx's materialism also has shortcomings. For one, economic relations cannot explain everything about society. Indeed, sometimes culture, art, consciousness, or new sets of political ideas emerge that cannot be directly explained by material factors. We saw this in chapter 1, in which cultural ideas about women's worth were made material in their diminished value on the labor market. In this example, cultural ideas are the cause of material conditions in labor markets, and not the other way around. Another example is the rise of fascism. Capitalist societies do not necessarily go fascist, but sometimes they do; whether they do or don't is dependent on a complex interrelation of factors, including material ones, such as the state of the economy and power of class relations, but also cultural ones, such as the degree to which workers believe and defend individual freedom and class solidarity and reject nationalism and xenophobia.[31] Racism is yet another example. Race relations and racism definitely have a material basis in capitalist societies, but undoing wage relations alone will likely not undo racist ideas and racist structures in society. Race and racism are cultural values that can operate independently of class and shape the class structure. So Marxist materialism is useful in many ways, but ideas and culture also seem to play a causal role independent of strict economic factors. Indeed, Marx's own analysis of the revolutions of 1848 reaches for extra-economic factors to explain exactly how and why the revolutions unfolded as they did.[32]

Even with shortcomings, these three ideas developed by Marx—alienation, surplus value, and materialism—go a long way toward helping us understand class. We've learned that class is embedded in economic and social structures of society; that wages and property are two sides of the same coin of exploitation; that workers trapped in this relationship are alienated from themselves and their labor; and that, to make progress toward human liberation, this entire structure, the wage system and property, will have to be undone. Many of these ideas were present in one form or another in socialist and even liberal thinkers years before Marx entered the scene. Marx had some unique expressions of these ideas, but for the most part his work became significant because he reinterpreted these works and established a powerful synthesis of anti-capitalist ideas.

Conclusion

Class and labor reside at the heart of both the political economy and underlying philosophy of modern society. From the advent of liberalism during the Enlightenment to the present day, ideological constructions of labor and work are at the foundation of justifications for both property and a vision of government designed to protect private property—for capitalist democracies. At the core of liberalism is the "labor theory of value," the idea that wealth, property, and profit are made possible by the labor of working people. For Locke, property is based on "mixing" one's labor with the natural world. And, whereas those who work industriously become their own justification for creating exclusion through private property, he also argues that wealth created through dependent labor and animal labor should accrue to the master. Others in the liberal tradition took the labor theory of value to its logical end. If one works the land, they are the rightful owner, and to deny workers the full extent of the value they create is wrong.

The socialist tradition breaks with liberalism over the question of property. Not only are the tillers and the renters the true owners of land, but the whole notion of property and ownership is faulty. Proudhon starts the tradition by highlighting the exclusive nature of property in that, by making private property, one necessarily takes from others. This kind of exclusion can only be justified by use, not mere ownership. Property therefore did not in fact reflect "ownership" but exclusion, the ability to prevent others from enjoying what is rightfully common. As such, property is at the core of how and why classes develop and are maintained in society. Proudhon tells us that property is theft and that private property, rents, and wages must all be done away with. Kropotkin goes one step further, arguing that all production and property is already "socialized" in modern industrial societies, part of a social network of production that makes individual demarcations of "property" meaningless. Instead, communism is best, a system in which "all is for all," and is one that reflects the already existing socialized nature of modern labor systems.

Marx built on and synthesized many of these ideas coming from the liberal and socialist movements of the nineteenth century. With alienation, surplus value, and materialism, he made important contributions. Workers are alienated from their work and from themselves; this is in part what makes labor exploitation possible through the extraction of surplus value. Marx was thinking systematically about capitalism, one of his greatest contributions. In his materialist conception of history, there are great insights about the relationship between material and cultural factors of society. But his argument that material conditions always "determine" history and culture was likely wrong, as we will explore in the next chapter. For now, let us leave Marx and the nineteenth century behind, and begin to think about how class was thought about and culturally constructed in the twentieth.

Chapter 4

Culture

In her critique of materialism, anarchist and revolutionary Voltairine de Cleyre writes that, according to materialist doctrine, ideas are seen as powerless. According to materialism, ideas are "impotent to determine the actions or relations of life as the image in the glass which should say to the body it reflects: 'I shape thee.'" Although the development of materialism was useful for correcting the faulty idealist worldview, she writes, "also there is a limit [to its power]." In the era of industrial capitalism, she suggested, human thought was dominated by the idea of consumerism, an idea she characterized as "thing-worship," or alternatively the "Much Making of Things." The implicit critique of materialism in her work is that the mere availability of material means does not make their use inevitable. Instead, materiality has to be employed through ideology—in this case, the ideology of "thing-worship"—to make mass production possible. De Cleyre points out that, in some instances, ideology and culture, as causal factors, trump materialism. Yet instead of recognizing this complexity, materialist teaching "is that ideas are but attendant phenomena."[1]

Since her writing in the early twentieth century, one strand of materialism has argued that ideas, like images in a mirror, had limited independent power to change society. But is this the case? De Cleyre was not alone in asking this question. Many other leftist thinkers began to challenge the orthodoxy of Marxist "scientific" materialism. Early critiques from anarchists and Marxists alike confronted the "empirical" predictions by Marx that had aged poorly; specifically, in the twentieth century, the working-class revolution was not looking "inevitable" but ever more distant. With the advent of social democracy and fascism as new forms of capitalist governance, working-class revolutionaries and thinkers had to recalibrate their emphasis on materialism. Instead, racism, nationalism, and progressivism were making themselves material through the application of state power. In response to fascism, revolutionaries looked to culture, to nationalism, to ideas, to explain the rise of the far right and failure of libertarian socialist movements. Later, intellectuals such as E. P. Thompson and Stuart Hall took culture and consciousness as their main starting points, showing how both culture and materiality are needed to explain class, social power, and the course of history.[2]

This chapter continues the development of ideas about class by exploring the critique of materialism and the advent of cultural understandings of class before transitioning to the intersectional concepts of racial capitalism and social reproduction in the next chapter. It argues that material and cultural factors are important components of class and that both are needed to properly understand class formation. Although materialism provides useful insights about how economy and social structure make history, particularly about how politics and ideas are shaped by class interests, it is an incomplete picture. If we consider the concept of "social totality," we can better see that materiality is but a piece, maybe a big one, of many social factors that contribute to history and social causality. We argue that intersectionality is more elegant a theory if we think of culture and materiality as co-constitutive; one way to see the "interlocking" forms of oppression is to look at how their composition is both material and cultural, economic and social. Indeed, to think of these factors as separate is an abstraction. As we hope to show, considering the social totality, material and cultural factors make each other, with materiality being defined by the structure of culture, and vice versa. This interaction helps us see intersectionality in a new light, one in which class, race, and gender truly co-construct one another.

If we take a focused look at culture, as we do in this chapter, it has its own "structure" that shapes history, society, and class. The structure of culture can be found in the deep and hidden meanings of language, embedded social practice, ideology, and expectations of behavior and human relationships. Jamaican theorist Hall pointed to these processes as something he called "articulation," the idea that social phenomena such as class are composed of the specific forces and contexts, both material and cultural, in which they operate. In contrast, British historian Thompson demonstrated how people become conscious of these forces in historical process. Both thinkers considered themselves of the materialist tradition and grew out of the Marxism discussed in the previous chapter. Crucially, both writers pointed to culture as an important, co-determinant facet of class and part of the process of class formation.

Limits of Materialism

Almost immediately after his death, but particularly after the death of Friedrich Engels in 1893, Marx's ideas were debated vigorously in the socialist movement. Materialism became so fundamental to socialist politics that to question or challenge it meant almost certain ostracism from the movement. Few critiques were raised from communists. But anarchists and others raised many questions early on. The basic critique was that the economic "foundation" of the Marxist theory is as much culturally constructed as it is a material phenomenon. Culture can make itself material through the practice of the law and the state, or by acting as important ideological or structural constraints that shape and guide people's understandings and actions. By the late nineteenth century, it was clear that the dogmatic adherence to materialism was in need of revision.

The first substantive critique of materialism came from Eduard Bernstein, a German social democrat and close confidant of Engels. Starting in the 1890s, Bernstein indicated that many of Marx's predictions about pending social revolution and the inevitability of the fall of capitalism and dictatorship of the proletariat were not coming to pass. If anything, things were pointing in the opposite direction, an opening of the political realm as a field of struggle and the ability to win real gains for working people through the political mechanisms of social democracy. Bernstein hoped to make Marxism more akin to the physical sciences, by which social theory was tested against an evidentiary base. Without evidence of the immediate advent of working-class social revolution, the claims of Marxist materialism had to be questioned and its content modified for it to remain a viable social theory.[3]

Bernstein found that historical materialism was lacking in several ways. For one, in its more rigid expressions, as the discussion of Marx's materialism in the previous chapter illustrates, it almost completely removes human agency from causality. Bernstein writes that, in determinist materialism, "Human beings are regarded as nothing but the living agents of historical forces whose work they carry out against their knowledge and will." Even in instances in Marx's writing of people coming to consciousness of revolutionary struggle, it is merely a consciousness of the material conditions they face, and, "all in all, the consciousness and will of human beings appear as factors decidedly subordinate to the material movement." In this vision, other forms of consciousness and understanding are false and don't contribute to the historical process. But this can hardly be the case. Ideas shape the world in important ways, and that shaping is done through concerted human effort, even if wrongheaded. Instead of materialism's structural emphasis, Bernstein argues that human agency is important; the actions we take and the ideas we hold can push against, alter, or radically transform the economic structures we are confronted with.[4]

Bernstein was writing to retain the value of materialism. In it he saw great use and explanatory power. A reformed "historical materialism by no means denies the autonomy of political and ideological forces," he writes, "it denies only that this autonomy is unconditional and shows that, in the end, the development of the economic foundation of social life—the relations of production and the development of classes—exercises the greater influence." But Bernstein is correct to point out that economic causes do not in any way "determine" how or why certain ideas take off and spread in a given society. He writes that economic causality doesn't determine the history of ideas, it only creates a "disposition for the reception of certain ideas." Ideas can then take on a life of their own, as how they "arise and spread and what form they take depends on the participation of a whole range of influences." This is to say that material conditions cannot account for and explain every aspect of the great variety and development of ideas and ideology. Partially for this mild and reasonable critique, but also for his political reformism, Bernstein was excommunicated from the circle of European Marxism in the twentieth century. His very name became a watchword of political "deviationism" and an affront to Marxist orthodoxy.[5]

Marxist materialism also found critics who challenged both its label as a "scientific" form of social inquiry and its reliance on "dialectics," the idea that all things contain contradictions within themselves. One such critic was the anarchist Warlaam Tcherkesoff, who in his 1902 *Pages of Socialist History: Teachings and Acts of Social Democracy* disputes the idea that Marxism was founded on "scientific" principles and rationale. "How can it be seriously maintained," he asks, "that sociological laws as exact as those of attraction and gravitation have been yet discovered, and that it is to Marx that we owe these 'discoveries'?" Instead, materialism and Marxism were not sciences akin to physical sciences but theories about society and causality that were sometimes right and sometimes wrong. He was especially heated in his condemnations of Marxist dogmatists for their belief in "dialectic materialism." "What a monstrosity," he exclaims, when dialectics as pure metaphysics with "no connection with science" claims an empirical, scientific foundation in materialism. The combination of the two, dialectics and materialism, Tcherkesoff argues, is not a leap forward but a leap back, an expression of ideology rather than a profound insight into the methods to understand society.[6]

Perhaps the best expression of the critique of "scientific materialism" comes from the anarchist revolutionary and working-class scholar Rudolf Rocker. A Yiddish language journalist and editor, Rocker was interned in wartime British concentration camps for his anarchism and opposition to World War I. Rocker writes in his work *Nationalism and Culture* that the failures of historical materialism were harming the revolutionary movements of the twentieth century. Written in 1937 on the eve of the World War II, Rocker was trying to explore why fascism had come to the fore at the moment that it did. If anything, the collapse of capitalism in the Great Depression was an opportunity for a leftist revolutionary breakthrough of the type Marx had always predicted. If ever there were a time for the inevitable rise of workers' revolution and the socialist society, this was it. Instead, the opposite happened: state capitalism gained ascendency, whether fascism in Europe, authoritarianism in Russia, or New Deal Keynesian economics in the United States and Great Britain. Rocker found that the "iron laws" of economics were not so iron or law-like after all. Instead, people's consciousness, ideas, culture, and ideology mattered; they could have a big impact, as big as economics, and sometimes were more determinative than material factors.[7]

Like others, Rocker found that the study of human society is not akin to the study of natural sciences. It therefore cannot possibly produce laws that can "determine" or "predict" certain sets of outcomes. Causality in social studies is very difficult to identify because society itself is so complicated. Rocker writes, "There is scarcely an historical event to whose shaping economic causes have not contributed, but economic forces are not the only motive powers which have set everything else in motion." So, yes, economics matter, and material structure is important, but there are other factors at play too. Looking for a causal relationship—what process "determines" the other—can be very difficult based on the complexity of social relationships. Rocker writes, "All social phenomena are the result of a series of various causes, in most cases so inwardly related that it is quite impossible clearly to separate one from the other." Instead, "We are always dealing with the interplay of various causes which, as a rule, can be clearly recognized but cannot be calculated according to scientific methods." Therefore, the notion that materialism is a scientific intervention like physics does more harm than good. If we want a more accurate understanding of society and history, rigid materialism must be tempered with nuanced thinking about social formation and causality.[8]

This critique of materialism based on the complexity of social relationships is a valuable contribution. But there is another ground for Rocker's critique; human will and agency play an important part in causality. "In social events," writes Rocker, "it is always a matter of a causality of human aims and ends, in nature always of a causality of physical necessity. The latter occur without any contribution on our part; the former are but manifestations of our will." Based on will, desire, calculation, conscious thought, and unconscious thought, individuals and societies could not be reduced to singular factors such as economics. Instead, material factors themselves were composed of cultural and social components. Rocker says that "religious ideas, ethical concepts, customs, habits, traditions, legal opinions, political organizations, institutions of property, forms of production, and so on, are not necessary implications of our physical being, but purely results of our desire for the achievement of preconceived ends." Here Rocker presents the idea that even material structures are a reflection of ideas, desires, and will, created for human interests, and hence changeable through human agency.[9]

The emphasis on human agency over dogmatic materialism is important. It returns revolutionary potential to the course of human affairs through a recognition that even fixed social structures are the result of human construction and can be shaped by concerted activity. For the worker, Rocker says, "Every form of his societal existence, every social institution which the past has bestowed on him as a legacy from remote ancestors, is the work of men [sic] and can be changed by human will and action or made to serve new ends." This emphasis on human agency, will, and consciousness allows us to shape and influence the economic and other structures of society with collective action.[10]

Rocker and others show us that dogmatic adherence to materialism has negative political implications. Rather than open up liberatory possibilities, dogmatic materialism forecloses options in people's minds, acting as a conservatizing force when applied in the arena of politics. Rocker explains that materialism is a "fatalistic" conception that can "only result in crippling men's power of resistance . . . consequently making them receptive to a compromise with given conditions, no matter how horrible and inhuman they may be." He argues that everyone "knows that economic conditions have an influence on the changes in social relations" but that "how men will react in their thoughts and actions to this influence is of great importance . . . in determining what steps they may decide to take to initiate an obviously necessary change in the conditions of life." In short, materialism needs to be radically rethought to account for a more complex social reality and for a more promising political practice.[11]

Class Formation: Consciousness, Experience, Dialogue

By the 1960s, Marxists were developing their own critiques of materialism and its relationship to class. The most significant was the work of Thompson, who wrote about the creation of the English working class. His 1963 book *The Making of the English Working Class* is a widely influential work to this day and the touchstone of the whole field of labor studies. Thompson took the consciousness of workers as the point of inception for class. He asked how consciousness and ideas were shaped by experience and events in a reciprocal process of class formation he called "dialogue" that combined materiality, consciousness, and agency. For Thompson, a historian, this is inexorably a historical process and contingent on social context. Nothing is guaranteed; there is no ensured or "inevitable" course of history and no singular consciousness that workers necessarily possess as a result of their conditions. Instead, to paraphrase Marx, working people make their own history but not so under the conditions of their own choosing. Thompson contributes to our discussion by showing how ideas, consciousness, "make" class happen as much as material factors. He writes convincingly about a process of class formation, an interplay between consciousness and the material factors of economics and social structure.

For Thompson, class formation is what happens when material conditions and consciousness align, when workers recognize and articulate a collective interest and take action to influence the course of events. In short, class formation is a process of coming to class consciousness. But because class is a complex and historically contingent process, there is no one class consciousness to come to. Instead, class formation reflects a process in which specific historical conditions, ideas, events, politics, and experiences contribute to new forms of understanding regarding the nature of class society. For example, in chapter 1, we saw how working women in textile factories in Lowell came to class consciousness infused in their identity of the "factory girl." For them, opposition to wages, loss of control of labor, and working like a machine combined with challenges to the "domestic sphere" ideology and patriarchal forms of control of women. This new consciousness fused into a movement of strikes, protests, writing, and resistance. Although there were other components of the process we didn't explore, such as an articulation of a revolutionary tradition of the American anticolonial revolt against the British, and components of racial formation around whiteness, all these factors contributed to their consciousness in a process we call class formation.

It was Thompson who first introduced this idea of class formation, and the clearest expression of his philosophy comes in his 1978 work, *The Poverty of Theory*. Ostensibly a defense of Marx's theories of history, of materialism, Thompson lays out a radically altered vision of materialist conceptions of history. In Thompson's version, culture, ideas, and consciousness are in reciprocal "dialogue" with material factors. Indeed, all of class formation can be seen as the social manifestation of the link between these two—both material and cultural. Thompson's presupposition is human thought; thinking agents experience the world, reflect, and redirect their actions and activities, thus both being shaped by and shaping the world. For Thompson, the crucial link comes in "experience" and the unfolding of history as a process, as history and experience are the basic "raw material" for both social theory and social change.[12]

His basic idea is that "experience" is rooted in human perception and in structural events and occurrences. People experience an event, reflect on it, and go on to shape future events. In his more poetic moments, Thompson writes that historical experience "does not wait discreetly outside" the office of history, "waiting for the moment at which the discourse of the proof will summon it into attendance." Instead, experience "walks in without knocking at the door, and announces deaths, crises of subsistence, trench warfare, unemployment, inflation, genocide. People starve: their survivors think in new ways about the market. People are imprisoned: in prison they meditate in new ways about the law. In the face of such general experiences old conceptual systems may crumble and new problematics insist upon their presence."

As prisoners, we meditate on the structures of law and markets; as survivors, we reconsider and alter the systems and conceptions that do not serve us. It is experience, as a historical process, not as an abstract phenomenon, in which thought, will, consciousness, structure, and materiality all come into contact and "determine" history and society. People can think and act, and sometimes do so in dramatic ways; experience makes this synthesis possible. So, when social changes "give rise to changed *experience*," Thompson writes, that "experience is *determining*, in the sense that it exerts pressures upon existent social consciousness, and proposes new questions."[13]

The interrelatedness embedded in experience is an important part of Thompson's second key idea, "dialogue." Here Thompson is talking about a relationship, a dialogue, between material factors and consciousness. Economics, social structure and class influence and change how people think. We enact those thoughts in practice that go back and shape social structure, and then are rearticulated in new thoughts and "problematics." Thompson writes that, between the material and ideological, "this dialogue goes both ways," in that "thought" becomes "being" and vice versa. Consciousness, he says, "whether as unselfconscious culture, or as myth, or as science, or law, or articulated ideology, thrusts back into being in its turn: as being is thought, so thought also is lived—people may, within limits, *live* the social or sexual expectations which are imposed upon them by dominant conceptual categories." In this lived experience, both material and cultural factors are at once at play. To take his example, expectations of sexuality are lived by those who've internalized those values. In that sense, they are material; they are a practice. Thompson argues that to attempt to disaggregate them results in foolhardy abstractions. Consequently, materiality and culture are fused in reciprocal dialogue. "We cannot," he writes, "conceive of any form of social being independent of its organizing concepts and expectations, nor could social being reproduce itself for a day without thought." The core of Thompson's concepts of dialogue and experience is that structure and agency, materiality, and consciousness are mutually reinforcing and historically contingent social forces.[14]

This is indeed a radical reformulation of Marx's materialism, one that finds antecedence in Marx's more nuanced historical work.[15] It is also completely at odds with Marx's rigid writings about historical materialism. Thompson situated himself in the Marxist tradition while arguing that the stern materialist dogmatists should be expelled. Indeed, Thompson rather expressly declared "unrelenting intellectual war against such Marxisms." Surely, he argues, the two cannot be properly housed in the same philosophical tradition. We agree, but it seems that Thompson is the one who broke with tradition, as the responses to his work from others in the Marxist school argued.[16] In fact, Thompson declares his intellectual work here in line with "libertarian communism," a phrase that he used to distinguish himself from the authoritarianism of Stalinism and related communisms as they developed mid-century. But it is also one that places him in the libertarian socialist tradition and, given the long history of similar critiques coming from anarchists and others, one he can rightly claim.[17]

What does this mean for our understanding of class? Thompson illustrated the application of this framework in *The Making of the English Working Class*. In that work, Thompson hoped to show in fine historical detail the process by which classes come into being. For Thompson, class is not defined as "a 'structure,' nor even as a 'category,' but as something which in fact happens . . . in human relationships." It is a process, one in which human experience and consciousness are at continual interplay, one that must be seen as historically contingent. He writes, "Like any other relationship, [class] is a fluency which evades analysis if we attempt to stop it dead at any given moment and atomise its structure." To do so, he continues, is to reveal "simply a multitude of individuals with a multitude of experiences." In this vision, class is necessarily an abstraction, a tool of analysis; it is partially made up of consciousness, of how we see and think and understand ourselves and our relationships. In the last analysis, class is composed of ourselves.[18]

For Thompson, if we allow ourselves to abstract a bit from individual experience and look to patterns of history and social relations, we can begin to see how class operates in capitalism. In his study of the English working class, for example, workers came to see an antagonism of interests between owners and workers as a fundamental component of wages and property, as we explored in chapter 1. So, for Thompson, "Class happens when some men, as a result of common experiences (inherited or shared), feel and articulate the identity of their interests as between themselves, and as against other men whose interests are different from (and usually opposed to) theirs." Class, then, is a process of developing collective interests with clear antagonisms, but one that must be collective and made conscious through experience. Therefore, looking to collective patterns of social relations, as agents or students of history, class emerges as a consciousness and articulation of these interests, relationships, and patterns. It is in this process of dialogue between structure, experience, and consciousness that class is made. Thus, in his famous articulation—"The working class did not rise like the sun at an appointed time. It was present at its own making"—class is not a material thing but a process of social formation in experience and coming into consciousness that makes class "happen."[19]

Thompson's framework in both *Poverty* and *Making* opened up new avenues of study, exploration, and practice. In addition to material factors, consciousness and culture emerged as key components of class composition. Upon this modified basis, many new insights and frameworks came into play, ones that dramatically improved the tradition of class studies and revolutionary struggle. For Thompson, class is an abstraction, and it is rooted in material conditions. Key here is the "permanent antagonism," or the opposed set of interests based on relations of property that we've explored earlier. But these factors are less meaningful without their conscious articulation by working people. Thompson provided a synthesis of material and cultural factors. Yes, relations of property, wages, and opposing interests all matter. But they can only take us so far in our understanding of class. Equally important is how people think about those relationships and interests, and how they experience and act on them. When these align, in lived history, we have class formation and a more meaningful way to understand class as a social phenomenon.

Culture: Structure and Articulation

Whereas Thompson sought to trouble Marxist materialism with an increased emphasis on consciousness and human agency, Stuart Hall introduced ideas of culture as important parts of class formation and capitalist structure. Hall was an intellectual who pioneered the field of cultural studies. He framed his intellectual journey and the founding of cultural studies as an explicitly political project and argued, with some of the critics of rigid Marxism before him, that the prediction of class struggle and world revolution were not borne out in history. Further, his work shows that there are some fundamental problems in how Marx conceptualized the base/superstructure model. Hall's basic argument is that, in the mid–twentieth-century era of affluence, in which consumers became an important part of capitalist economics, culture shaped class formation and the capitalist "totality" in important ways.

Hall begins with the some of the critiques we have already seen, that the rigid construction of Marx's base/superstructure model is flawed. One way Hall explores this is by showing that the base is actually more complicated than simply consisting of economic factors. Borrowing from literary scholars, Hall shows that, in thinking about an economic base, "it is impossible to give an account of the mode of production without taking cultural definitions into account." His basic point is that, if the "base" is meant to give us an understanding of how humans organize their material existence, there is no way to understand that organization without thinking about how humans prioritize, value, and give meaning to the material world and their needs in it. This is to say that ideology and cultural understandings profoundly co-determine what the "material" is; attempts to bifurcate them or show a unidirectional "determining" relationship from the base upward are faulty. In short, Hall argues, "There is no way of describing the economic life without reference to the cultural forms in which it is organized."[20]

By way of example, Hall explores the relationship of law to the economy. The regular functioning of markets, corporations, profits, and exchange all rest on the capacity of the law—part of the "superstructure"—to make those practices possible. One specific example Hall draws from the work of Marx and Engels themselves is the nineteenth-century British factory laws. Working conditions in early industrial production were extremely poor, and working-class peoples launched social movements to change their conditions. The result in England was the passage of a series of "factory acts" starting in the 1830s and continuing throughout the century that sought to improve the working conditions of the class. Children were forbidden to work, safety and sanitation standards were imposed, and minimum wage and maximum hour limits were created. The construction and enforcement of these standards changed the functioning of the economy and the structure of labor markets. For example, children below a certain age were prohibited from contributing to labor markets. For Hall, this shows how classes—and here he meant the working class and not the "dominant" class—used "ideas and practices of reform to impose limits on a particular tendency in the mode of production." Similarly, with laws criminalizing homosexuality or marijuana use, we can see the cultural values being made material without a singular factor of economic determination at play.[21]

A second important idea from Hall is that culture has a structure. In the social sciences, "structure" is a concept that denotes the types of institutions, organizations, and arrangements that give form to a particular society. The term is a metaphor borrowed from biology, in which the "structural" functions of a cell, and its ribosomes and mitochondria, can be compared to the structural organization of a society, such as the law, markets, family, or social relationships. Social structures, then, are important pillars and frameworks that make particular social formations possible and set limits on what is achievable under those conditions. In relation to concepts of class, we can say wages or markets constitute the structure for parts of society, guiding available pathways and directing people toward particular experiences and outcomes. Borrowing from cultural philosophers Raymond Williams, Claude Lévi-Strauss, and Émile Durkheim, Hall developed a notion of the structure of culture. And much like social structure, cultural structure can also set limits, orient behavior, and create possibilities and outcomes.[22]

Hall's notion of the structure of culture looks to linguistics, anthropology, and literary studies to think about how concepts and cultural practices make up the social formations of class. In a very basic sense, this is the idea that social norms and expectations set and delimit forms of acceptable and expected behavior from individuals and groups. But, borrowing from anthropologists, Hall goes on to show how people "impose a system of meaning" on the world around them. The material world doesn't have intrinsic meaning or comprehensibility. Instead, we impose systems of order, categorization, and intelligibility on the world to make sense of our experiences and observations. We can think of this as how people imagine "natural" or "real" social relations such as the family, gender, race, or class. There is no necessary "real" or inherent construction of masculinity, for example; rather, people perceive particular types of behaviors or norms as what defines the role of "men." These can have important impacts on social institutions such as kinship, work, and policing. In this way, according to Hall, culture "structures" the society we live in and experiences we have. It therefore also shapes the formation and meaning of class and other social relationships.[23]

But to look at the "deep structure" of culture we need to make use of theories about language, ideology, and symbolism. Language and ideology can so deeply shape our mental constructions of the world that they influence how we act and relate to the material world without us knowing, becoming like a material structure itself. A core concept about how linguistic structure affects culture and worldview comes from the linguistic anthropologist Benjamin Lee Whorf. Using his experience as a fire-prevention engineer, Whorf began to see that "purely physical" fire protections were only so effective; equally important were the ways that language shape our consciousness. In a famous example of "empty gasoline drums," Whorf explained that culture and language itself can be the cause of fire. Drums void of liquid gasoline still contained vapors, and the English word "empty" can't adequately reflect a complex reality of drums that once contained liquid gasoline, no longer do, yet still contain dangerous vapors. Here the word "empty" imposes a meaning on the world that is not wholly accurate and shapes human behavior around the drums that leads to potentially explosive outcomes. Whorf's basic idea is that the deep structure of culture is contained in the linguistic practice and ideological formations that shape understanding and consciousness in ways that we may not even be aware of. This insight led to the famous Whorf thesis that "the structure of language influences thought processes and our perception of the world around us."[24]

Hall takes these ideas from structural and linguistic anthropology and applies them to thinking about class. He posits that, just as language can constitute a deep structure of culture, so too can ideology. Ideologies are "systems of representation," he says, that are made up of "concepts, ideas, myths or images" that people then use to construct "their imaginary relations to the real conditions of existence." The examples of race and gender are useful here, where we unknowingly construct expectations of behavior and relationships and mistake them for parts of the natural order. Once again, the concepts in our heads play an important role in structuring the material world. If the structure of language offers the building blocks of cultural structuralism, then ideologies act as the larger institutional forms that give culture its coherence and set specific limits as to what is possible.[25]

With this insight on the social constructedness of culture and meaning, Hall warns against the pitfalls of postmodern readings of language and culture. Although it may be tempting to say that if language and cultural practice are merely imposing visions of the world in ways that don't accurately fit reality, as in the example of "empty gasoline drums," then there is no "correspondence" between language and the real world, or any particular precise meaning. Perhaps all we can say is that language elides meaning and that there is nothing "real" to discuss anymore. Hall says that it is true that there is "no necessary correspondence" between language and meaning, but that doesn't mean that there is never any correspondence. Indeed, he argues that ideology operates by "fixing meaning through establishing, by selection and combination, a chain of equivalencies." Perhaps this chain of meaning-fixing doesn't align perfectly or at all, but in some circumstances it might, and in those instances it becomes possible to say something meaningful and intelligible and to intervene in the world in concerted ways. In short, although the insights of cultural studies have the power to pull us away from empirical reality, we should resist that temptation, as cultural structure and materiality should be thought of in conjuncture with one another.[26]

This leads us to Hall's concept of "articulation," which is when those notions and ideas, impositions of ideologies, are present by a shared context in a specific way that allows collective action to take place. Articulation is the process whereby cultural meaning-making align with specific historical conditions to make possible understanding, thought, agency, and, ultimately, political movement. So, when language, ideology, culture, politics, and economic conditions relate to each other in particular formations, gaining an understanding of world or making valuable meaning of the world becomes possible in new ways. In relationship to class, in the right context, "articulations between social groups, political practices, and ideological formations which could create . . . historical breaks" from the fixity of ideological or material structures are, in fact, possible. Therefore, articulation is an important insight that not only helps us to understand the process of cultural and material structure that bound our society, but also to take action to change and reshape them. This is a remarkably liberatory vision of social structure and collective action, and it is one that is important to any understanding of class.[27]

This brings us to a third important insight from Hall—the social totality of capitalism. Here Hall is most directly drawing from Marx's concept of the capitalist totality but also from Williams, the literary scholar, who argues that totality has important cultural dimensions as well. The notion behind social totality is that we can think of the individual structural components of social organization, whether material or cultural, as contributing to a comprehensive whole. This notion is helpful in that it allows us to see and reflect on the interconnectedness of social formations and think systemically about the types of social phenomena that we observe. In the makings of class, we can better understand that class is not simply an economic relation but also a multi-causal social phenomenon that is highly contingent. It is contingent on the social formations and context in which it operates and on the political, economic, ideological, and cultural forces that give it meaning. All this contingency and totality relates to what Hall calls "articulation." These factors may align to make class happen, but they may not. And, much like Thompson sees, class happens when a particular articulation of cultural and material forces within a broader social totality align.

To elaborate these ideas, Hall uses two examples: "Blackness" and religion, specifically the Rastafarianism of his home country, Jamaica. With religion, Hall tells us that religious belief and practice have no particular political or social content; their "articulation" comes from the array of other process and social forces around it. Rasta comes from a tradition of Christian cosmologies that are rearticulated in new contexts and with new purposes. Those new articulations include the emergence of a Jamaican underclass in the context of British colonialism and conceptualizations of the African diasporic movement. Rastafarianism then is a specific articulation of religion that is made meaningful in the social context in which it is produced and made legible. It is in part a class phenomenon, a social philosophy, a racial identification, a religious practice, and many other things. Most importantly, in this instance, religion contains elements of resistance and can be part of social movements of liberation. Indeed, when social movements, class, ideology, and religion are articulated in specific ways, this opens up the possibility of struggle that moves us toward liberation. When this happens in relationship to wages, property, and collective identity, we have a process of articulation that we can call class formation. Thus, for Hall, a structural understanding of the "totality" is not without conflict and contestation, as religion or other forms can be sites of social struggle.[28]

It is perhaps not surprising that Hall's primary example for thinking about articulation and the structure of culture was through his analysis of race, specifically his discussion of "Blackness." Hall provides the example of how his racial identity was articulated differently as he moved through different settings from Jamaica to the United Kingdom to the university. Hall notes that he had been variously identified as "coloured," "Negro," "West Indian," "Black," and "immigrant." How he was seen and identified relied on the specific types of contextual "articulations"—in part, cultural, material, and historical—in these different circumstances. For example, in Jamaica, he was identified as "coloured" to denote specifically how his light skin and class bearing meant that he was categorically not "Black." There, a Black laboring class was distinct from the kind of mixed-race, class-mobile background that he came from. When he moved to England, people on the street also identified him as "coloured," but there it had different meanings—specifically, to be identified as Black or as in relationship to Blackness. In the United Kingdom, this carried a whole different set of class, colonial, and gendered connotations—for example, being an immigrant and racialized member of the working class. We can say the same for his other forms of chosen and imposed identities, which can also become points of struggle. Hall points this out in relation to the contestation of the meaning of "Black," as the same term can have different cultural connotations and meanings based on the structured articulations of those places and traditions, and as those very concepts are open to the field of social struggle. Therefore, the social category "Black" or "coloured" itself has a class character and politics that are important to struggle over and define in social movement.[29]

To take just one example, the "Black is beautiful" movement demonstrates how social categories, identities, and definitions are not essential but instead are sites of political, class struggle. Once a term of derogation, in the hands of Black people active in movements for liberation, "Blackness" became a positive term, as with the slogans "Black is beautiful," "Black Power," and "Black Pride." But contained within the movement were gender and class struggles about defining Blackness in particular ways. Whereas debates about Blackness and beauty have been present since the beginning of modernity, twentieth-century movements were grounded in the rise of advertising and mass culture in the early 1900s. With the creation of mass consumer markets, white audiences were explicit targets of advertising, and white standards of beauty consciously and unconsciously reinforced in advertising materials. At the same time, African Americans were haunted by images from slavery and minstrelsy that depicted Black people with exaggerated and monstrous features. Some African-American beauty companies emphasized appearing more "white" using skin bleach and hair straighteners to combat these images. Others, such as those owned by Madam C. J. Walker and Annie Turnbo Malone, the first Black millionaires, saw beautiful Black features as markers of racial uplift; Black people, women in particular, should be proud and confident in the beauty of their own features and hair. At the same time, social movements such as Marcus Garvey's pan-African Universal Negro Improvement Association featured women with dark skin and natural hair in their promotional materials.[30]

By the time of the Black liberation movements of the 1960s, the "Black is beautiful" tradition was being radicalized and rearticulated in new ways. Natural Black hair, in the form of Afros, close cuts, cornrows, and other forms, became popular and powerful symbols of Black empowerment. This originated in a tradition of "bohemian" Black women intellectuals and artists who were trying to articulate Blackness in new ways. In the mid-1960s, Black radicals such as the Black Panthers adopted the fashion and changed the meaning of the Afro, associating the look with masculinity, radical anti capitalist pol itics, and resistance to white supremacy. Indeed, the power of the symbolism of Angela Davis's large Afro became an important marker in the public campaign to demonize her as a dangerous Black radical.

Even so, with time, natural hair styles such as the Afro were commodified and worked into a Black cosmetics industry that attempted to strip the radical politics from the style. Companies such as Clairol began marketing the "natural" look to Black consumers, framing the style as a choice of individual self-expression rather than collective resistance. In 1967, Clairol's CEO sponsored a Black Power conference in Philadelphia. This was not very different from the commodification of Black Pride in the 1910s and 1920s. Walker, in particular, became rich on her hair care franchise business rooted in networks of Black women's solidarity. The point is that the changing meaning of Blackness, through physical expression and personal style, was and is a terrain of contestation that fractures on gender, class, and other forms of social "articulation." What gives meaning to Blackness, the Afro hairstyle, whiteness, masculinity, or any other social form and identity is a political struggle and a class struggle that can be articulated in many different ways, both conscious and unconscious.[31]

With concepts such as class formation and articulation, any field can be opened to political struggle, and the work of Stuart Hall and cultural studies gives us some important insights for our thinking about class. From the basic understanding that the economic base is as much a cultural construction as a material one, Hall proceeds to explore how culture has its own operational dynamics that "determine" the scope of society and course of history in important ways. Consequently, we can say that culture itself has a structure. It is structured through the deep meaning of language, the hidden values of ideology, and the embedded practices of society that make themselves material in everyday life. Hall sees these practices as being "articulated" in specific, contingent, and contextual ways. When these intersections of meaning, structure, and materiality happen in just the right ways, we get the process of class formation. This understanding, in which structure and meaning are contingent and open to contestation, demonstrates the possibility of liberatory struggle against the systems that oppress us. And, as we will see in the next chapter, it is rooted and co-formed in constructions of race and gender. Hall's work helps us further our understanding of class as intersectional with race and gender and opens the pathways for liberatory movements now and into the future.

Conclusion

When de Cleyre wrote her critique of materialism in the early twentieth century, she condemned rigid materialism for holding culture and ideology as impotent social forces. In her metaphor, culture was merely a reflected image telling the body, "I shape thee," an absurdity in the materialist framework. But, of course, how we see and understand the world, the ideas we bring to it, both conscious and unconscious, do in fact shape our material reality. In the very structure of culture and in the agency we have in the face of powerful material and cultural structures, our ideas and consciousness matter. In this chapter, we've explored the critiques of dogmatic adherence to materialism, and how culture and consciousness are central to the making of class and its continued importance in contemporary politics. For Thompson, working people developed and articulated their own form of socialist politics as sophisticated as anyone's. But that process was contingent and historically shaped. It was in no way "determined" by the simple facts of their economic existence. Instead, people had to come to particular forms of understanding through struggle, politics, ideological formation, and the creation of culture—the process of class formation.

With this idea of class formation, Hall developed the concept of "articulation." This idea takes parts from materiality and culture, structure and agency, to show a complex process of class formation in all these dimensions. His work is also tied to the idea of social totality and shows how multiple factors, a complementary whole of social formation, goes into making something as complex as class. Both of these insights open the prospect of liberatory struggle, as even the deep material and cultural structure of society can be altered with concerted activity. As we will see in the next chapter, this improved understanding of complexity and multiple causality can help us with ideas coming from movement activists and scholars too. Ideas such as intersectionality, in which race, gender, and class are understood to be mutually constitutive, are greatly enhanced by ideas such as articulation and social totality, and by the synthesis of material and cultural factors. If class is a process of social formation, of articulation that is contingent on the social constructions around it, then so too are race and gender. Further, these articulations influence and shape one another in any given historical circumstance. Class is always racialized and gendered, and vice versa. It is to these forms of social articulation that we turn in the next chapter.

Chapter 5

Intersectionality

"We are actively committed to struggling against racial, sexual, heterosexual, and class oppression." The Combahee River Collective, an organization of Black feminists coming out of the movements for liberation in the 1960s and 1970s, wrote this as they began to articulate intersectional politics for the first time. Their efforts and the work of many others by mid-century show that the doctrine of Marxist class analysis was undergoing major reformulations. The notion that class was the "basic" or the "paramount" form of social exploitation and oppression was being radically rethought. More to the point, the very understanding of class, as solely materially determined, was losing credence. Instead, as social movements developed, people came to see problems of race, class, and gender as fused, as "intersectional," shaping and supporting one another. Social struggle was not just about material conditions or cultural forms but a synthesis of both, against multiple forms of oppression. The insights from Thompson, Hall, and others about the role of material and cultural forces were developed by and with working-class movements of Black radicalism, feminist materialism, and Black feminism, and the Combahee River Collective was just one of many pointing in a new direction.[1]

The collective statement was one of the earliest and remains one of the best expressions of intersectional theory that treats race, gender, and class as social systems that reinforce each other and require holistic movement struggle. "Based upon the fact that the major systems of oppression are interlocking," they argued that movement theory and organizing had to reflect that complexity, that intersectionality. Their focus on intersectionality echoed earlier notions of class-struggle feminists, such as those of Sarah Bagley and the factory girls, who dedicated themselves to "war with oppression in every form" as early as the 1840s. This chapter takes the material and cultural construction of class developed in previous chapters and shows how this more nuanced understanding of class formation complements intersectional theory.[2]

We can better understand the concept of intersectionality by using the ideas of materiality, culture, structure, agency, and totality that developed in previous chapters. Earlier we showed how culture shapes the material world, how it contains its own complicated structure based on language and ideology, and how, together with material factors such as wages and property, it contributes to a capitalist totality. In that complex whole, systems of race, class, and gender "articulate" one another, or are defined and constituted in relation to one another. With this conceptual footing, Black and feminist thinkers developed new analysis of social struggle and new visions of liberation. In the Black radical tradition, Cedric Robinson, C. L. R. James, and W. E. B. Du Bois highlighted the way the social structure of racism and the forces of capitalism reinforced one another in the experience of Black workers, a process Robinson called "racial capitalism." As he showed, this was not just a process acting on Black workers but was true at all times, and for white workers too, rooted in the structure of racial capitalism. Similarly, feminists looking for the root sources of sexism and patriarchy found parallel structures in class and capitalism, specifically around the control and exploitation of women's and workers' bodies. Black feminists showed how patriarchy, white supremacy, and capitalism are simultaneously material and cultural phenomena and mutually reinforcing structures of power that affect people differently. Together, these traditions produced intersectional theory, the ideas that different forms of oppression reinforce and construct one another.

Racial Capitalism

The originator of the idea of racial capitalism, Robinson, was born in

Oakland, California, in 1940, and was influenced by the experience of his grandparents. His grandfather had to flee Alabama after assaulting his wife's boss in self-defense, an incident itself at the intersection of white supremacy, capitalism, and gender violence. Robinson attended the University of California at Berkeley, where he became an activist and influential among the milieu that would go on to found the Black Panthers in 1966. His 1983 work, *Black Marxism: The Making of the Black Radical Tradition*, synthesized and identified a global "Black radical tradition" that included people such as C. L. R. James, Du Bois, and American novelist Richard Wright. His theory of racial capitalism emphasized the synthetic development of white supremacy and the advent of capitalism. As we've seen, class is a totality, both material and cultural. So too are systems of race and, in fact, white supremacy has its own material structures in the economy and cultural structures in society. Robinson's theory of racial capitalism helps us see that capitalism is inherently a racial project, and that the process of class formation explored in the previous chapters is simultaneously a process of racial formation.[3]

With racial capitalism, Robinson built on the cultural insights of Thompson and the tradition of Marxist historical materialism. Whereas Thompson was interested in the ways material conditions produced new and different forms of consciousness as workers encountered wages and industrial capitalism, Robinson flipped the model and explored how an ostensibly cultural phenomenon such as racism took on material aspects in people's lived experiences. Robinson's basic formulation is that the tradition of "racialism," of privileging racial or national identities, not only predated the rise of capitalism but also defined the emerging structures and material relationships of capitalism. In essence, he tells us, as "the development, organization, and expansion of capitalist society pursued racial imperatives, so too did the social ideology that grew up to defend capitalism." We can see this in the work of Locke, for example, who used racialized conceptions of the "wild Indian" to justify capitalism and colonialism's rapacious resource and labor exploitation; or in the English working class, who defined themselves as racially distinct from Irish workers. "As a material force," Robinson writes, "then it could be expected that racialism would inevitably permeate the social structures emergent from capitalism," a structure he calls "racial capitalism." In short, the structures and ideologies of race and class co-evolved.[4]

Robinson argues that, for centuries, European peoples developed concepts and practices of race in hierarchical social relationships. For example, he points to the German tradition of Herrenvolk and English Anglo-Saxonism as examples of ethnic and racial practices and hierarchies. These practices were embedded in the material organization of society and in the "traditions of consciousness" of how people understood themselves and their world. This "racialism" was transmitted through successive forms of social organization and was remade with the advent of the structures of capitalism. "Racialism," Robinson argues, "ran deep in the bowels of Western culture." He continues, "Racialism insinuated not only medieval, feudal, and capitalist social structures, forms of property, and modes of production, but as well the very values and traditions of consciousness through which the peoples of these ages came to understand their worlds and their experiences. Western culture, constituting the structure from which European consciousness was appropriated, the structure in which social identities and perceptions were grounded in the past, transmitted a racialism that adapted to the political and material exigencies of the moment."[5]

In this definition of racialism, Robinson builds from the ideas of Thompson and cultural studies, arguing that culture itself is a type of "structure" that shapes and determines the material world. Specifically, he argues that pre-capitalist and feudal conceptions of race influenced the creation of social relations of production in capitalism. This includes material forms, such as property, but also mental conceptions and consciousness, which have their own structure.

For evidence, Robinson turned to Thompson's English working class. He argues that, even in the "racially pure" circumstances of the emergence of the English workers, race was ever-present because of the social impact of the Irish. In the United Kingdom, the Irish became the cheapest and most exploitable workforce in part as a result of the history of colonialism. English attitudes toward the Irish as colonial subjects were akin to racism. They were seen as racially inferior to Anglo-Saxons and widely characterized as lazy, stupid, violent, and prone to alcoholism. For example, writing in the 1830s, the British writer and politician Benjamin Disraeli said that the Irish were a "wild, reckless, indolent, uncertain and superstitious race" with "no sympathy with the English character." Additionally, the Irish in England, fleeing the impacts of famine and colonialism, were destitute, impoverished, and desperate for work of any type. As a result, in Thompson's words, the Irish were "the cheapest labour in Western Europe." Irish workers then took "the heavy manual occupations at the base of industrial society [which] required a spendthrift expense of sheer physical energy." Consequently, English workers' conception of themselves as a distinct class was made in relation to conceptions of dependent Irish workers. In Robinson's summation, "the Irish worker having descended from an inferior race, so his English employers believed, the cheap market value of his labor was but its most rational form." Here racial attitudes about the Irish and the legacy of colonial occupation produced material effects in market prices for Irish labor.[6]

Robinson's point is that this type of racial formation was taking place at the exact same moment that Thompson's English working class were making themselves. For both groups, Irish and English, awareness of the other helped shape their class position and their consciousness of that position. The process of class formation in the English working class was simultaneously a process of racial formation in which some workers—even those facing similar conditions and with similar skin tone—were constructed as racialized "others," a group apart. This process of racialization was happening between peoples that modern readers would view as "white," demonstrating both that the process of racialization is ever-present with capitalism and the historical construction of race and its mutability.

A unitary, fused process of race and class formation, however, is not a factor only of pre-industrial history. We can take the insights of racial capitalism and see the intersection of these forces in the composition of modern labor markets too. Market competition, when applied to human labor, fosters animosity and division. For example, in capitalist competition over job placement, workers can come to see difference, frequently racialized, as an important mechanism for protecting privileged positions or preventing competition from diluting wage rates. This is most commonly reflected in the anti-immigrant racism present in virtually every industrialized nation. Here differences of national origin and identity are used as a wedge to limit labor supply and "protect jobs." But this structural competitive factor also reinforces restrictive and hierarchical conceptions of national identity and race. We can also see this in other forms of labor-market competition and racialization, such as tiered labor markets and racial violence and job discrimination directed against oppressed peoples. Racialization in labor markets is perhaps one of the best examples of the intersection made visible through the insights of racial capitalism.

Black Radical Tradition

The other major intervention of Robinson's work was to identify the "Black radical tradition," something he pieced together from the experience of Black struggle—in his words, "an accretion, over generations, of collective intelligence gathered from struggle." The key insight is that Black thinkers have not only identified the synthesis of race and class in forms of social oppression but have also developed means to struggle against them holistically, using labor as a fulcrum of power to fight slavery and white supremacy, or highlight and support race struggles such as those for civil rights as fundamentally class issues. The Black radical tradition shows us not only the intersections but also the methods of resistance.[7]

There is probably no more significant figure in the Black radical tradition than Du Bois. An American scholar from Harvard, Du Bois saw the Black freedom struggle as entwined with class struggle. His greatest work, *Black Reconstruction in America: 1860–1880*, argues that the American Civil War and end of slavery were triumphs of the self-activity of the southern Black proletariat. Du Bois treated slavery as a system of labor and showed that the slave system was ultimately undone in the United States not by presidential fiat but through the collective work and action of enslaved peoples themselves. As the war unfolded, Black workers, enslaved people, refused to support the Confederacy. They fled plantations and flooded Union lines in the hundreds of thousands. Direct resistance by enslaved people eroded the southern economy and therefore the Confederate war effort, draining the South's ability to fight. Black workers also forced the issue of slavery onto northern political agendas. It became clear that undermining Confederate labor systems was the key to winning the war, and President Abraham Lincoln soon called for the emancipation of southern slaves. White southern workers also came to see that their interests were not tied to the planter class and refused labor and military service, resisted, or fled in other ways. This collective resistance Du Bois called a "general strike," an economic activity with dramatic racial consequences for generations to come. Du Bois argues it forced both the end of slavery and the military victory of the North. But it also shows us the complicated interpolation of race and class, and that movements for Black liberation can win through labor.[8]

Du Bois's primary concern in Black Reconstruction is not slavery and the American Civil War, but the end of the period of federal reconstruction that followed the war. Reconstruction, Du Bois argues, was a moment of real possibility for Black Americans. Backed by federal power for its own reasons, African Americans participated in political activity in a way that had never been possible before. Its end spelled disaster for Black America and is explained by the exigencies of the southern class system. In the aftermath of the war, the South was completely destroyed, including the economy. White landowners tried to get Black labor back on the plantation; they did this through force and violence, in some respects taking on the dynamics of full-scale war. The process was called "redemption." It forced southern Blacks into agricultural work in a system known as sharecropping, and it stripped them of political rights through the imposition of "Jim Crow" segregation. For southern Blacks, this meant extreme poverty, racism, and terrorist violence.[9]

What is more, during redemption, the imposition of the structures of white supremacy hurt white people too. In Louisiana, for example, redeemers cut taxes on the richest residents, and they cut social programs that most benefited newly freed African Americans, such as schools and public hospitals. They also made it very difficult to vote, passing laws that required literacy tests, poll taxes, or complicated legal scholarship. The purpose of the legal attacks was to limit the power of African Americans and restrict them to a condition as close to slavery as possible. In their pursuit of white supremacy, the racist elites of the Louisiana dragged down the social position of poor whites too. As Black workers were disenfranchised, so too were white workers; Black voting rolls were reduced by more than 100,000 in a very short period, but poor whites unable to pass literacy texts or other restrictions were also reduced by 80,000. As public schools were cut and closed, Black literacy declined by the end of the century, but so too did white literacy, as fewer whites could read at the end of the century. These changes targeted African Americans and hurt Black workers more, but white workers also fell victim to gross injustice of institutionalized white supremacy. By 1892, the working class of New Orleans, Black and white, had had enough; despite efforts to divide them, they staged an interracial general strike that won many improvements for Black and white workers. Employers tried to break the strike by making appeals to race hatred in the press, but the workers held firm. Black and white workers supported each other to win a shorter workday and better working conditions, things that benefit all members of the working class, Black and white.[10]

Besides Du Bois, there were other thinkers who contributed to the Black radical tradition, C. L. R. James among them. James, a Trinidadian émigré to the United States and United Kingdom, was a reformed Marxist who came to see cultural factors such as race and white supremacy as important structural components. His main contribution was integrating Black experiences into Marxist thought, and he came to believe that the programs of socialism, on their own, were insufficient to support Black liberation. In a famous conversation with Bolshevik revolutionary Leon Trotsky in the Coyoacán area of Mexico City, James argued that struggles around Black liberation, or for civil rights in the United States, for example, were part of the class struggle and needed to be developed on their own terms. His most famous work, *The Black Jacobins*, demonstrated that the enslaved people of Saint-Domingue (Haiti) were more like a working class because of their labor conditions in which large gangs worked in intensive output. It was those horrific labor conditions that gave rise to the Haitian revolution. But, of course, the revolution was a race war too. And because the French colonial ruling class was white, the intersections of race and class were clearer to see. Much like Du Bois, James took the lived realities of Black workers as the starting point and came to see race and class as fundamentally intertwined. For James, within systems and histories of colonialism, the intersection of race and class was very clear.[11]

James's most significant work in this regard is his article "The Historical Development of the Negro in the United States." Writing pseudonymously in 1943, James argues that the Black struggle in the United States, even when based in the expansion of bourgeois democracy, is an example of class struggle because of the relationship of African Americans to class and capitalism. He frames his argument against two materialist, class-reductive arguments—one that sees African Americans as a separate national entity within the United States and another that argues that the struggle against racial oppression has to be subordinated to the class struggle. Instead, James argues that Black peoples' "struggle for democratic rights brings the Negroes almost immediately face to face with capital and the state" and that therefore "this struggle is a direct part of the struggle for socialism." Even when based on a civil rights footing, in a fight strictly against American racism, the Black struggle was a class struggle. James shows us that, because of their "proletarian composition," their working-class character, African-American social movements for freedom challenged the state and capital and therefore were the leading edge of class struggle in the United States.[12]

Another scholar, Martinique-born philosopher, psychiatrist, and revolutionary Frantz Fanon, also focused on the intersection of race and class in the colonial experience. Fanon engaged with Marxist conceptions of base and superstructure; like many of the thinkers we've explored, he saw shortcomings in Marxist theory. For Fanon, in the French colonial experience, "the economic substructure is also a superstructure." As he explains, race and class reinforce one another: "The cause is the consequence; you are rich because you are white, you are white because you are rich." Fanon explores the psychological impacts of such a social order based on white supremacy and capitalism, and the necessity of violence as a form of anticolonial struggle. For our purposes, in both the lived experience of Caribbean Africans and in the nature of the colonial project, race and class were fused and self-reinforcing structures of social power. Although it's possible to imagine the two as analytically distinct, this is not how they developed in historical process and lived experience. The bedrocks of colonialism are capitalist exploitation and white supremacy; if we try to divide the two in our analysis, we impoverish our understanding. For Fanon, it was therefore necessary to "stretch" Marxism, specifically the materialist interpretation, to account for more social complexity in the colonial experience. With Fanon, C. L. R. James, and Du Bois, we can see an emerging tradition that places cultural, material, racial, and economic forces in mutual constitution.[13]

With these insights from the Black radical tradition, we can better understand our own history and current circumstance. The subordinate position of Black workers in the United States continued well into the twentieth century. The major reforms of the century, those of the New Deal in the 1930s, encoded Black economic disfranchisement into law. When the federal government passed legislation making unions legal and providing worker protections, African Americans were written out of the law. Southern Democrats wanted to keep Black workers outside of federal protections, and created exclusions for agricultural and domestic workers, then 90 percent of the Black workforce. These laws are still in effect, although with impacts on different groups of racialized workers now, mostly Latin American immigrants. Although the New Deal reforms were a major benefit to white workers, Black workers were again intentionally left out. The result was to further entrench the tiered labor market and race/class relations in the United States. Through much of the twentieth century, this bifurcated labor market, with Black workers and people of color relegated to worse social positions, would continue. This is racial capitalism, whereby a culture of racism produces material reality.[14]

Some of this came to be undone through the civil rights movement, which frequently also recognized the synthesis of race and class and often fought for economic rights alongside political rights. For example, the highpoint of the civil rights struggle, the 1963 March on Washington, in which Martin Luther King, Jr. delivered his famous "I Have a Dream" speech, was a march for "jobs and freedom." Even though the march was for economic and political gains, a recognition of the intersection of race and class, the economic aspects of the civil rights movement are often ignored in our narratives of the Black freedom struggle. But King and others continued to recognize the intersection throughout his life; in fact, King was killed at a strike, supporting sanitation workers in Memphis, Tennessee. His widow, Coretta Scott King, went on to fight for the "full employment" bill to ensure Black economic enfranchisement. And civil rights groups in the North, such as the Congress of Racial Equality (CORE), fought to integrate jobs, to create access for Black workers to new sectors of employment, and for improved housing conditions. We can again see this with the emergence of "Black Power," in which economic self-determination was a core demand of the movement.[15]

After winning significant political victories, King told Congress in 1966, "We see economic issues as the basic issue." Yet one major space in which the civil rights movement failed was in winning lasting economic victories. Political rights came, but they proved ineffective at fundamentally changing the position of Black workers in the structure of American capitalism. Some, very few, individual Black figures were able to gain wealth and transcend class limitations. For the majority of Black workers, after a brief window of opportunity, the tide was turned, and many of the underlying economic conditions have remained unchanged.[16]

Materialist Feminism

Much like those in the Black liberation movement who found in the materialist tradition a useful tool to understand racial capitalism, so too parts of the feminist movement quickly developed a synthetic relationship with class analysis. Materialist feminists working at about the same time developed new insights about the condition of women in the capitalist world. They focused on Marx's concept of "social reproduction." If the goal of capitalism is to produce commodities for profit, then a key need is to produce people, as laborers or consumers, to make profit possible. Social reproduction emphasizes the ways that the "production of people" in capitalism is gendered, in that the work of care is structured as unpaid women's work. This unpaid work is at the intersection of gender and capital and is a core component of profit-making; it is made possible by the efforts to control women's bodies. Social reproduction theory is an important contribution to our understanding of the capitalist "totality"—or what others have called the "social factory"—the place where we are produced to further capital, at the expense of women's autonomy and self-control. In this metaphor, all of capitalist society is one big profit-making machine, or big factory, and we should consider its individual components such as housework and caring labor as part of the totality.[17]

The early figures who emphasized work and labor in the tradition of feminist thought was Selma James and her co-author, Italian intellectual and revolutionary Mariarosa Dalla Costa. Brooklyn-born Selma James dedicated her life to the movement for liberation and revolution, becoming a partner and working comrade with C. L. R. James. Selma James and Dalla Costa's emphasis on work as a dimension of women's oppression was a critical insight. Their 1972 text "The Power of Women and the Subversion of the Community" is a profound argument for the synthesis of gender oppression, class exploitation, and racism, and gave the cultural analysis of women's oppression a "materialist" grounding in labor. But Selma James and Dalla Costa did not want to simply affix women's struggle as an appendage of the class struggle—they saw the two as part of a complementary whole. In their words, they wanted to reject "on the one hand class subordinated to feminism and on the other feminism subordinated to class."[18]

For Selma James and Dalla Costa, labor was key, and women's social condition was explained by "the unwaged housework assigned to us . . . this work produced capital's entire labor force but was not even considered work." This unpaid work is tied to powerlessness in other social realms. They write, "Unwaged work is the basis of our powerlessness in relation both to men and to capital." This central injustice meant that women's labor-market value was undercut, producing lower wages when they did enter the workforce, and that women's domestic work was devalued too, creating dependence on men. James and Dalla Costa focused on unpaid reproductive work, on housework, because most women were subject to household exploitation regardless of whether they had paid employment.[19]

This emphasis on work provided a number of important conceptual and political insights. For one, unpaid labor, in effect, provided capital a huge and ongoing basis for profit accumulation. Historian Jeanne Boydston studied how women's unremunerated work underwrote capitalist profits. In her detailed study of American women of the industrial working class, she found that unpaid women's labor contributed $100 million to capital accumulation in the early nineteenth century. Women's scavenging, food procurement, taking boarders, or sex work undoubtedly supplemented wages that were below subsistence levels. For women, this relationship meant a kind of double dependency. Whereas men who were workers were dependent on the wage, women were dependent on men who were wage workers. If they lost their relationship with men, they faced economic destitution and poverty. Here the wage, a social ill in its own right, also dramatically strengthened the relations of patriarchy. As Selma James argues, "Precisely through the wage has the exploitation of the non-wage laborer been organized." And this continues to the present day. A *New York Times* article from 2020 places the figure of unremunerated reproductive work at $10.9 trillion annually. Women's unpaid work was and is a core social division, one based on illegitimate hierarchy and power that predated the emergence of capital and capitalism, and that helped give support, both material and ideological, to labor regimes such as wages.[20]

If all of society is structured to facilitate profit accumulation, then struggles in all segments of society are struggles against capital. Conflicts outside the workplace, in the home, in the community, in schools and theaters and parks, are part of what Selma James calls a "capitalist totality" based on the "total social labor." Therefore, political contestations over rent, "transport, housing, medical care, education, the police, are all points of struggle," all tied to class and feminist struggles. Household fights for power therefore are simultaneously about patriarchy and capitalism. Selma James and Dalla Costa call the conceptual framework they used to understand this relationship the "social factory." The concept of the social factory is important because it helps us understand how conflict and contestation that we may experience as individual or personal (e.g., who picks the kids up from daycare or who does the dishes) are conflicts that are structured through capitalism and therefore part of the class struggle. In light of the intersectional theory we are using here too, these struggles are also raced and gendered, part of the social totality, social factory. Importantly for us, the social factory imbricates all social struggle with the class struggle, the feminist struggle, and we should add the struggle against white supremacy.[21]

There is one other important point from Selma James and Dalla Costa. If the source of women's social disempowerment was unwaged work, then the source of their power was to reclaim control of that work. One way to do this came in the "wages for housework" campaign. This campaign highlighted the degree of unremunerated work that contributed to capitalism, and it tried to make the capitalist state account for the cost by paying those who did the work. This campaign was launched in the early part of the twentieth century by women socialists and again later in the century during the so-called second wave by materialist feminists including Selma James and others. The clear hope was that wages for housework would break the double bind of working-class women. On the one hand, it would help liberate them from waged work by paying them for work they already did, thus alleviating downward pressures on the labor market. On the other hand, it would break the dependence of women on men by providing a level of economic independence. Wages for housework aimed to force capital, through the state, to pay for the true costs of their production, something that could contribute to weakening the political strength of capital. Reclaiming control of work, of labor, for women and all workers, is a vital source of social power in systems based on the exploitation of that labor. Selma James and Dalla Costa write that "refusing to *work* is a fundamental lever of social power."[22]

Although James and Dalla Costa were primarily concerned with the condition of unwaged working-class women, as we have already seen, many women, even at the origin of industrialization, were waged. For these women, a whole set of working-class feminist politics emerged that were in fact distinct both from those of the labor movement and the mainstream middle-class feminist movement. As historian Dorothy Sue Cobble explores, working-class women employed in paid labor and using their unions as tools of struggle often developed ingenious methods of resistance to empower themselves and better their class position. One was special protections for women in the workplace, measures seen as retrograde now. Working-class women fought hard for hour limitations and workplace safety measures based on their special status as women. Women in the labor movement also fought for equality, for things such as equal pay for comparable work, for access to traditionally "male" jobs, and a wage standardization based on job placement and seniority. This was a struggle for both equality and special treatment, an important tension to keep in mind as we move the struggle for human emancipation forward. As Cobble explains, "Theirs was a vision of equality that claimed justice on the basis of their humanity, not on the basis of their sameness with men."[23]

From this grounding in labor and work, later feminist thinkers came to see other parallels in both capitalism and patriarchy and developed Marxist conceptions of "social reproduction" through an emphasis on controlling workers and women's bodies. A key figure here is Silvia Federici, an Italian and American academic and activist who in her book *Caliban and the Witch* argues that women's social subjugation is more than simply a cultural or material force, that capitalism and patriarchy are fused at the hip, and that women's liberation is part of a revolutionary struggle to undo class and capitalism.

One of Federici's insights comes from thinking about capitalism's need to control bodies. She and other feminists argue that Marx's idea of social reproduction needed to be developed and that his focus on production missed the crucial element of how workers produced themselves. In the case of the wage worker, as we saw in Lowell, capitalist production meant the loss of control of one's body while on the job. Federici's argument is that, as capitalism seeks to control workers' bodies in production, it also needs to control workers' bodies in reproduction. In societies with a gendered division of labor, this is women's work, and it means controlling women's bodies outside of paid work. "Along these lines," she writes, "the body has been for women in capitalist society what the factory has been for male waged workers: the primary ground of their exploitation and resistance, as the female body has been appropriated by the state and men and forced to function as a means for the reproduction and accumulation of labor." By not paying women for the necessary work that it takes to make profit possible, capitalism seizes from women value they create. To make that happen, systems of controlling women's work and bodies, a system of patriarchy, is a necessary part of capitalism.[24]

According to Federici, the notion that it is possible to separate patriarchy and capitalism in our analysis is faulty. Her work seeks to break down "the dichotomy between 'gender' and 'class.'" Her first insight is that, with a sexual division of labor, gender is in part defined by "work-function," and therefore a core component of class formation. She writes, "If 'femininity' has been constituted in capitalist society as a work-function masking the production of the workforce under the cover of a biological destiny, then 'women's history' is 'class history.'" Like the Black radical tradition did with race, Federici argues that gender oppression has a fundamental class element and simultaneously that capital is inherently gendered. "Gender should not be considered a purely cultural reality, but should be treated as a specification of class relations," she argues. Because the work of social reproduction in the domestic sphere is a core defining component of femininity, constructions of gender inherently have a class composition.[25]

Federici emphasizes the continuing role of violence against women and shows how the need to control women's bodies extended into the need to control reproduction. For example, in the early fifteenth century across Europe, a very ugly conflict emerged as a nascent form of capitalism sought to wrest knowledge and control of women's reproduction and sexuality away from them. Federici says that the witch trials, a violent expression of patriarchal control, were necessary to take this power away from women and transform their labor, reproductive and otherwise, to meet the goals of capital and patriarchy. This process, Federici argues, did not stop with the termination of the witch hunts. Using violence to control women's bodies became an enduring feature of capitalism and patriarchy, something with us to this day, through conflicts over access to reproductive health care, abortion, domestic violence, and femicide. In the works of Federici, we see that the structural need to control women's bodies for profit accumulation is enforced through violence and rigid gender roles.[26]

With working-class feminism, a few key insights emerge. The first is that capitalism and patriarchy are fused in the effort to control working women's bodies. The need for unpaid "social reproduction" and the gender division of labor means that women's work, necessary for the profitability of capitalism, needs to be controlled and unremunerated. At the base, control is achieved through violence, and the ongoing struggles of women against patriarchal violence are tied to these deep social structures. Unpaid women's work also means that women are dependent on men wage earners, and that their market value is undercut by the large volume of unpaid work produced on a daily basis and the pervasive cultural devaluation of women. This means that struggles in the home, struggles for state-provided childcare, or struggles for paid housework are all part of the combined class struggle and feminist struggle against the capitalist totality. The final key insight is that this picture of class struggle is not one of universal interests. Instead, the class is multiple and diverse, and the cause of freedom and equality may not be achieved through blanket equality. Instead, real equality reflects the diversity and specificity of our conditions and experiences.

Black Feminist Thought

Contributing to this work, Black women theorists and revolutionaries produced intersectional theory through struggle and critical reflection. Marginalized by social movements and targeted by multiple structures of power, Black women wrote early about the intersectional nature of social power and oppression. Based on experience and identity, those who developed the tradition of Black feminist thought argued that there was no singular experience of women, of Black people, of workers. Instead, difference, diversity, and contestation defined them all. They understood how the articulation of race, class, and gender reinforced one another, and how their struggle against any one of these instantly imbricated them in the others. Whereas Black feminist activists in the Combahee River Collective first started to articulate these concepts, academics such as Kimberlé Crenshaw introduced the term "intersectionality" to highlight the co-composition of oppression. (Although, as "intersectionality" has been used, it is frequently missing a class component, as discussed in the introduction.) Whether we use the language of intersectionality, social totality, or complementary holism, the idea that these social forces need to be understood in relation to one another came from Black feminist thinkers. They came to articulate collective experience that could adequately grapple with internal difference as the core of what made social categories meaningful.

Perhaps the clearest, certainly one of the most famous, expressions of this analysis came in 1977 with the statement by the Combahee River Collective that opens this chapter. The document was intended to solidify some of the tenets of Black feminism, and as such defined the history of struggle of Black women as connected to both the tradition of feminism and the struggles for liberation from patriarchy, and the Black liberation movement and the struggle against racism and white supremacy. Important for us is that the Collective included their class politics, their socialism, and their opposition to capitalism, placing themselves in the tradition of intersectional class struggle that we have been exploring in this work. They wrote, "Sexual politics under patriarchy is as pervasive in Black women's lives as are the politics of class and race. We also often find it difficult to separate race from class from sex oppression because in our lives they are most often experienced simultaneously." Their key contribution was with identity and experience. In the lived experience of Black working-class women, the systems of patriarchy, white supremacy, and capital were fused. In some ways similar to Thompson's use of "experience" explored in chapter 4, for the Collective, identity emerged as a way to understand the intersections of these systems.[27]

The "Combahee River Collective Statement" was part of a much broader intervention by Black feminists on the importance of intersectionality going back hundreds of years. One of the earliest articulations of this position, and perhaps the clearest, comes from Sojourner Truth. Truth escaped slavery in New York to become a tireless organizer for liberation. It was at an Akron, Ohio, women's rights convention that Truth gave her most famous address, the 1851 "Ain't I a woman?" speech. Although the specific text of Truth's speech may be apocryphal, her ideas make it one of the richest and most compelling documents in the history of U.S. politics. In it, Truth makes a radical claim for equality across difference and brings race, class, and gender into her field of analysis in the cause of human liberation. Addressing a man who argues that Truth not be allowed to speak at the convention, Truth simultaneously breaks down and makes a claim to the social category of "woman." "Look at me," she demands, "look at my arm! I have ploughed, and planted, and gathered into barns, and no man could head me. And ain't I a woman?" Here Truth is making a claim on class, on her former status as an enslaved person and a worker. This status, she argues, doesn't diminish any claim to "womanhood"; in fact, it strengthens it.[28]

Truth's speech gives a radical formulation of womanhood, a vision of equality that embraces difference. She makes this claim most strongly when she discusses "intellect." In her rebuke to the argument that women, African Americans, or workers shouldn't be included because of diminished intellect, she rejoins that, even if so, that is a case for an expanded role of freedom of action, not a diminished role. "If my cup won't hold but a pint," she asks, "and yours holds a quart, wouldn't you be mean not to let me have my little half measure full?" Truth is likely using a rhetorical ploy here and not actually making a claim about intellect. Instead, Truth's argument is that the equality of scope of freedom is demanded not by the equality of condition or characteristic, but on the need for a recognition and expression of difference. Truth's claims on both womanhood and intellect show that, even with difference, freedom is a requisite, and social categories such as "woman" still cohere. I may not fit your mold, but ain't I a woman too, she asks. And so too with class, in which working-class people may not work in a factory, or even receive a wage, yet they are still members of the class because of their relationship to property, their social relationships, their race and gendered subjectivities, et cetera. Although the experiences, needs, and interests of women, workers, and their claims to freedom may be wildly different, we still fit and can make claims on the basis of our experiences, social categories, and identification.[29]

The work of Angela Davis carried on Truth's intervention. Born in Alabama during World War II, Davis went on to become a radical scholar. She was dismissed from her position at the University of California at Los Angeles for her politics and persecuted and jailed for over a year before being acquitted for her movement participation. Davis's body of writing, particularly her book, *Women, Race, and Class*, places the experience of Black women at the center of her analysis to explore the intersection of capitalism, patriarchy, and white supremacy. Moving through the literature on slavery, the women's movement, labor, and immigration, Davis makes the case that the experiences of women, workers, and African Americans are routinely ignored, but that they play a central role in the foundation of systems of oppression. For example, her review of the literature on slavery highlights that enslaved women were routinely excluded by historians even though Black women were at the center of these systems. This was true in the women's movement too, in which both Black women and working-class women's perspectives were excluded from the vision and histories of the white-dominated feminist movement. By looking to the exclusion and the marginalization, Davis showed a more complete picture of the whole.[30]

Davis's work on difference within movements and between social positions of women continues the work of Truth and others in breaking open social categories of analysis. For example, in her discussion of the women's movement of the nineteenth century, Davis highlights that the perspective and voices of Black women and enslaved women such as Truth, and waged working-class women such as those of the Lowell factory girls, were excluded from the demands of the movement. So, instead of seeing the abolition of slavery and an end to wages as feminist demands, they are seen as marginal, derivative, or secondary, belonging to other movements. Women's demands for the vote, divorce, and property rights, although important claims on their own, are reflective of middle-class needs and do not make up the plurality of experiences that constitute the social category of "woman."

This is a useful insight for our work on class. Much like there is no universal position that can define or signify "woman," there is also no universal position that can constitute "working class." Instead, a multiplicity of perspectives, voices, and experiences, at times very different from one another, constitute what it means to be a woman. Even with this plurality, Davis and others never take their focus off the social system that makes these categories meaningful. Although there is a plurality of experiences, there are systems of patriarchy and wages that enforce certain shared conditions. Therefore, although the category of woman may be multivalent, it is still significant and an important site of struggle to level specific fights around. This is true for class too. Although there is no universal class experience, there are structures of class with a multiplicity of experiences that still make the category viable.[31]

Another scholar in this tradition is the writer and activist Patricia Hill Collins. Her work develops a theoretically rich concept of intersectionality that we can draw on to better understand class. One way that Collins does this is by demonstrating the relationship of heterogeneous collective experience to make the tradition of what she calls "Black feminist thought." For Collins, there is no "essential" Black women's experience. It is defined by the intersection of race, class, and gender, and the variety of individual experience and consciousness within that matrix. In this thinking, structure and condition shape individual experience and consciousness, but there is no one-to-one correlation because we are all unique, thinking beings. Although we may have similar experiences, we often draw different conclusions from them. In her words, "No homogeneous Black *woman's* standpoint exists." Rather than a singular, "Black women's" perspective, it is through a collectivity of individuals and experiences that a position like "Black feminist thought" can emerge. With a multiplicity of voices, we get a better understanding of the whole. This collective process, with an emphasis on difference and intersection, is more a methodology, a way of seeing. And it is especially true because the conditions and experiences of Black women are constantly undergoing change, from slave labor to waged domestic labor to contemporary forms of exploitation, displacement, and violence.[32]

In the work of Collins, much like Thompson, the historian of the English working class, the process of experience, thought, and action is a dialogical one; it is about the relationship between each in part of the larger process. And Collins highlights the necessity of collective endeavor to make the process meaningful. She writes that a "collective group consciousness dedicated to resisting oppression becomes possible" only when "individual expression of consciousness are articulated, argued through, contested, and aggregated in ways that reflect the heterogeneity of Black womanhood." Importantly, these are processes that must be self-articulated and self-defined. They cannot be imposed from without or constructed in a way that excludes or mitigates the plurality of experience. Collins and others emphasize the importance of shared experience but highlight that there is no universal consciousness or politics that emerges from a shared structural position. Instead, diversity, difference, disagreement, and collective process are central to the theory and methodology of Black feminist thought.[33]

What emerges here is a working-class politics and culture worthy of the name. It is the beginning point in creating a class for ourselves. In the intersectional and process-oriented politics of Black feminism, we can see material, cultural, personal, collective, structural, and individual factors all at play. This is the culture, consciousness, and politics of class struggle. Yes, we have important differences, but we also cohere into social categories formed by social structure from which it is difficult to escape. If these categories don't define us, they certainly define our struggles for liberation, as the structures must be undone for us to be truly free.

Conclusion

Following the American Civil War, at the end of Reconstruction, in the South white supremacist parties won election victories and seized state power through violence. In the North, industrial capitalism syphoned European immigrants into a rigid and violent industrial order. A century later, people's historian Howard Zinn reflected on those changes to American society. For him, the legacy of the era was a "skillful terracing," a class structure infused with race, gender, nationality, and other markers of difference. "In the year 1877," he writes, "the signals were given for the rest of the century: the black would be put back; the strikes of white workers would not be tolerated; the industrial and political elites of North and South would take hold of the country and organize the greatest march of economic growth in human history. They would do it with the aid of, and as the expense of black labor, white labor, Chinese labor, European immigrant labor, female labor, rewarding them differently by race, sex, national origin, and social class, in such a way as to create separate levels of oppression—a skillful terracing to stabilize the pyramid of wealth."[34]

The skillful terracing of oppression that Zinn observed emerging after Reconstruction is with us today. It is a class system that has been co-formed with systems of white supremacy, patriarchy, national exclusion, and other forms of oppression. This system is part of a complementary whole, a "capitalist totality," in which structures of race and gender define class just as much as one's relationship to the means of production. With the benefit of hindsight, Zinn could see the contours of our modern class system emerge, but he was not alone recognizing these changes. The philosophers and activists of the Black radical tradition, working-class feminists, and Black feminists all express core insights of the intersectional class-struggle tradition.

By the time of the freedom movements of the 1960s and 1970s, a more complex and holistic picture of class began to emerge, one that took into account the lived and varied experiences of a diverse working class. From Black theorists such as Robinson came the notion that capitalism was in fact racial; it was and always will be a material and cultural construction he called "racial capitalism." For feminist scholars and activists, a core element of patriarchy was also class exploitation; the two were inseparable wholes. Feminist scholars including Selma James and Silvia Federici developed concepts such as "the capitalist totality" and the "social factory" to explore how class and capitalism touch virtually all of our lives. They also showed how the exploitation of work and working bodies underpinned capitalism and patriarchy. Black feminists taught us the importance of intersectionality, and of difference and heterogeneity in our self-definition and our movements for liberation. Together, these thinkers offer us a compelling portrait of how class is both a shared structural experience common to all and lived through particular forms of oppression and difference. This skillful terracing is something we all share a collective interest in undoing, even as it impacts each of us differently.

Chapter 6

Practice

In the late 1970s, toward the end of the Cultural Revolution in China, the programs of the Maoist government were failing and China was coming to a historic crossroads with its revolutionary tradition. The intelligentsia and political class worshiped "Mao Zedong Thought," and questioning the teachings and ideas of Mao was unmentionable in public. One philosopher and revolutionary, Hu Yaobang, felt trapped in the rigidity of this intellectual environment. He called this worship of Mao's teaching "whateverism"—whatever Mao had said and taught must have been correct. Looking around, he saw that the teachings of Mao had caused significant human suffering and were leading to a dead end. He penned one of the more famous articles in modern Chinese history, titled simply, "Practice Is the Sole Criterion of Truth." Without directly criticizing Mao, Hu argued that theoretical insights of Maoism were failing in the lived experience of Chinese people. Instead, for theory to be proven correct, it must be tested in practice. The relationship of theoretical truth to real-world practice is a useful insight that unfortunately in China was used to open the door to the market reforms of the Deng Xiaoping regime and a long slide toward contemporary Chinese state capitalism. Nonetheless, the key theoretical insight of Hu rings true and is the measure of this chapter. The theory of intersectional class struggle we've helped piece together in this work is not worth much if we can't see it put into practice.[1]

Thankfully, intersectional class struggle is very much a living tradition and has a long history of practice. The struggles explored in this chapter demonstrate the insights of intersectional class struggle put into practice in working-class movements from around the world. If we take these ideas to heart—articulation, the social totality, materialism, difference, and intersectionality—they can help us see the connections in our oppression and provide pathways to liberation. In the field of anti-racist struggle, in both the abolition of slavery and the end of apartheid, class intersectionality shows where power lies to dismantle the structures of white supremacy and how to build mass struggle across racial divides. This is the case as well in movements focused on gender, ecology, and immigration, in which a combination of different sectors of the class become active and the use of mass direct action demonstrates class power in practice. In these examples, the power found through workplace struggle has been crucial to create movements that have the ability to topple the core institutions of oppression. This is a central part of building popular power and is especially true when different sectors of the class—workers, students, soldiers, homemakers, the unemployed—come together in mass movements to challenge concentrated power. Creating directly democratic working-class organizations not only challenges oppression but also makes new institutions and social relationships that we can use to pivot away from capitalism, white supremacy, patriarchy, and colonialism, and to create a new society.

When we say with Hu that the ultimate criterion of truth is practice, we mean that intersectional class struggle has to be tested through practice and that the ideas are nothing if not made real. Thankfully, they are continually put into play all around us in the movements and structures of power arrayed against them. The more we are aware of these connections, and act on them, the stronger our movements will be and the closer we will be to collective liberation.

Anti-Racist Class Struggle

As we've seen with the "general strike" of enslaved workers during the American Civil War, class power is an important lever to break forms of social oppression that might otherwise remain immutable. What the example of the enslaved workers' general strike shows is that a small minority, for whom white society cared very little except as a source of profit, had the power in their labor to achieve the unthinkable—completely destroying slavery, the core institution of American racial capitalism. More than this, as W. E. B. Du Bois and others argued, the labor power of enslaved workers was the key to winning the war for the North too, eroding the ability of the South to fight and turning the tide for the Union. My point regarding the "general strike" of enslaved workers during the American Civil War is that the oppression and exploitation of African Americans in the United States was intersectional in the structure of American society, embedded in both the culture and economy of white supremacy. Therefore, the resistance necessarily had to be intersectional, taking on the race and class dynamics of slavery if it hoped to achieve liberation. Enslaved people held power in their labor, and it was by withholding their labor that they were able not only to improve their working conditions but also to challenge white supremacy, transform the structure of society, end slavery, conclude the war in victory, and contribute to a more humane world.[2]

Whereas labor-power was key to undoing slavery, it was also key in the struggle against South African apartheid. In 1973, the labor movement in the working-class port city of Durban organized a general strike that set the stage for the struggle against apartheid by building power on the job. In the 1960s, South African racial capitalism was booming, largely on the backs of low-paid Black workers who had their unions outlawed and faced extreme forms of disfranchisement through the apartheid system. In 1969, and again in October of 1972, Black dockworkers struck to demand higher wages and better treatment. Their efforts were largely successful, resulting in wage gains and, as historian Peter Cole argues, they were the immediate catalyst for the Durban Great Strike started just weeks later in January 1973. The Durban Great Strike saw 100,000 workers walk out of their jobs for better pay and better treatment but, most importantly, it gave workers the experience of self-empowerment against the ruling structures in South Africa. In the strike's wake, workers had increased legal coverage to organize unions and strikes, and they used that ability based on workplace power to level a decades-long fight against the apartheid regime. According to the South African Online History project, the 1973 Durban Great Strike "signaled the central role of working class organizations in shaping the ideology, strategy, and tactics of the struggle against Apartheid and racial capitalism, which culminated in the fall of the Apartheid regime in the 1990s." As with the demise of U.S. slavery, labor-power was key in demonstrating popular power that Black South Africans held to undo the systems that oppressed them. [3]

If class struggle contributed to the end of slavery and apartheid, it can provide the foundation for anti-racist struggle to thwart white supremacy too. In the 1930s, a new type of union, an "industrial" union that welcomed all workers in a single workplace, emerged as the cutting edge of working-class struggle. Previously, unions and employers both had a long history of racism and support for white supremacy. Certain jobs were reserved for whites, and Black workers were kept out of factories and union halls. This had catastrophic consequences for the working class. For example, in the 1919 Steel Strike, employers brought in 30,000 Black and immigrant workers to break the strike staged by white workers and their racially exclusive unions. Long prevented from joining those unions, and the labor movement in general, Black workers crossed the picket lines. With that, employers got production moving again, defeated the strike, and prevented worker organizing for the next 15 years.[4]

In the 1930s, as the labor movement thought about how to win during the Great Depression, the lessons of the 1919 Steel Strike loomed large; workers' movements would have to be anti-racist and intersectional if they were to win. The strength of the model of industrial unionism was that it required overcoming racial divides within the workplace. New organizations, such as the Congress of Industrial Organizations (CIO), ran anti-racist trainings to facilitate Black and white workers organizing together to fight employers. It formed interracial social groups and sport teams, challenged public displays of racism, and highlighted the treatment Black workers faced on the job. This was largely the influence of the communist and other leftist organizers in the union, for whom anti-racism had long been part of their practice of labor organizing. But at its core were the ideas that Black and white workers have a common enemy in capitalists and capital, and that efforts to divide workers by race weaken working-class power. With these union campaigns, along explicitly anti-racist lines, unionization at places such as General Motors in Flint or in the mills of U.S. Steel finally became possible.[5]

In the estimation of Du Bois, the CIO was one of the most successful anti-racist efforts in U.S. history. "Probably the greatest and most effective effort toward interracial understating among the working masses," he writes, "has come about through the trade union." He believed that shared class interests were a mechanism to overcome ingrained racial hostility. Because of the CIO, workers "in the steel and automotive industries have been thrown together, black and white, as fellow workers striving for the same objects. There has been on this account an astonishing spread of interracial tolerance and understanding." Those victories breaking down white supremacy were won through intersectional class struggle; in Du Bois's words, "Probably no movement in the last thirty years has been so successful in softening race prejudice among the masses." Black workers were harmed the most by racism and white supremacy, but white workers were harmed too as their unions were broken and their living standards eroded by taking the side of employers in supporting white supremacy against working-class solidarity. In short, all workers have a collective interest to overcome white supremacy and labor-market competition together. In practice, this often means prioritizing the Black freedom struggle or movements for civil rights to build that solidarity.[6]

Like these other examples, the contemporary struggle against incarceration and police violence is intersectional. In Michelle Alexander's book on mass incarceration, *The New Jim Crow*, Alexander links the issue of policing and American racism, the fact that the capitalist incarceration system disproportionately detains and imprisons people of color, to the class stratification of American society. She argues that the modern incarceration system is but the latest manifestation of a centuries-long process of enforcing a permanent Black underclass in America. As a lawyer, Alexander's emphasis is on voting and restrictions to civic participation. But in her work it is clear how mass incarceration, as well as the systems of Jim Crow and slavery, have much broader impacts on the Black working class and on the class as a whole. Incarceration is a mechanism of social control: it permanently disrupts one's ability to work, disrupts family relations, and isolates and alienates people from one another. For Alexander, mass incarceration is an appendage of the capitalist state that enforces a rigid structure of racial class stratification.[7]

In another example of the power of labor to challenge white supremacy, in Florida in 2018, prison workers struck for a month to refuse poor conditions and unpaid work, which they called "slave labor." Similar strikes in California and other states led to a nationwide prison strike later that year. Focusing on their labor, a major source of their power, prisoners were able to challenge the prison-industrial complex, one of the major institutions of white supremacy. With this emphasis on labor and direct action, intersectional class struggle strategies benefit social movements and group empowerment even far from the traditional workplace. They also show how to address complex intersections of state power, white supremacy, and capitalist exploitation.[8]

In all these examples, the structure of Black oppression is indelibly infused with the class structure. In her book, *From #BlackLives-Matter to Black Liberation*, Keeanga-Yamahtta Taylor explores the origins and causes of the Black Lives Matter movement. She argues that at the root of the "black awakening in Obama's America" was a class-stratified Black community. Those better suited to benefit from the legacy of the civil rights movement were able to integrate into U.S. ruling circles, such as the Obamas, Powells, Whartons, and others. The rest of Black society was left behind, increasingly criminalized, and given over to neoliberal policies that left communities to deal on their own with gripping poverty and militarized policing amid the war on drugs. The result is that Black protest bubbled up from the bottom. Through direct action, mostly riots and disruptive protests such as blocking freeways, the movement was able to force the issue of deadly policing onto the national agenda. In some instances, it was able to win important gains, such as limiting police access to military hardware.[9]

This is not to say that race is fundamentally all about class. It is to say that these issues are intersectional—and not just between race and class. For example, police violence is also gendered, as the routine violence exhibited by police officers is a deadly manifestation of "toxic" masculinity. It is gendered too in the relative invisibility of the women and trans people killed by police violence. As Keeanga-Yamahtta

Taylor argues, without a grounding in emancipatory revolutionary class politics, it is unlikely we can adequately address the racism and injustice of police violence and other issues that concern us.[10]

Working-Class Feminism

Working-class intersectional feminism has long argued that women's exploitation is rooted in both material and cultural factors, and it has put forward programs that contribute to liberatory movements. For example, in the 1970s, many socialist feminists, Selma James and Silvia Federici among them, fought for a "wages for housework" campaign. As we saw in the preceding chapter, the idea behind the campaign—that housework was work and should be remunerated—was rooted in social reproduction theory. Every day, millions of workers prepare their clothes, make their lunches, wash their dishes, and commute sometimes very long distances, all of it unpaid, just to make it to a job. The social factory argument they used suggests that these processes contribute to employer profit accumulation and, as such, should be paid. Paying all people to do this work—but primarily women who are customarily responsible for it—would have many benefits for the working class. It would be a direct assault on the power of capital to externalize costs, and it would empower those without a wage outside of the workplace. For example, people who may be tied to abusive relationships or other dangerous circumstances because they lack the material basis to support themselves would have better leverage to leave. Wages for housework therefore could undo imbalanced gender dynamics and empower labor at the bottom of the gender hierarchy. As James and others rightly argued, just highlighting the issue, running the campaign for wages, makes visible a whole segment of labor currently made invisible as the natural way of things. What working-class feminism shows us, then, is that women's oppression is intersectional in practice and that the movements of resistance recognized this and created intersectional campaigns to break the hold of both capitalism and patriarchy.[11]

Intersectional gender liberation includes sexual liberation too, and the LGBTQ+ movement has its origins in intersectional struggle. The Stonewall Riot in New York in 1969 is one such example. After a police raid on a gay bar in the Greenwich Village, gay, lesbian, and trans activists, many of them people of color and many facing homelessness and poverty, revolted against police arrests and harassment. Criminalization and the psychopathology of homosexuality in the 1960s meant that gay people in the United States had to live a life undercover, "in the closet," and could be punished if they were openly gay. At clandestine clubs, police routinely arrested adults for consensual sex. The Stonewall Riot is commonly portrayed as a spontaneous uprising of fed-up queers who took to the streets out of rage and hope—an "outburst of desperation and vengeance." This is partly true, but many of the leading rebels were longtime activists and revolutionaries who were radicalized in the feminist and anti-war movements of the 1960s and carried an intersectional practice with them into the streets. Some of the leading organizations of the era, including Street Transvestite Action Revolutionaries (STAR), DYKETACTICS, Gay Liberation Front, Third World Gay Revolution, and the Combahee River Collective, all expressed intersectional politics and framed gay liberation within a social movement ecology of anti-capitalist, anti-racist, anti-imperialist, and feminist organizing.[12]

STAR, for example, founded by trans activists Sylvia Rivera and Marsha Johnson, was created by and for "street gay people, the street homeless people, and anybody who needed help at that time." People were shunned from families and unable to find traditional employment outside of sex work, and poverty, homelessness, and economic precarity were rampant in the New York gay and trans scene. These issues were explicitly addressed in the Third World Gay Revolution's 16-point program, which included planks for "the right to self-determination over the use of our bodies: The right to free physiological change and modification of sex on demand, . . . liberation for all women . . . [and] guaranteed income or employment, regardless of sex or sexual preference." The contemporary trans and queer movement carries these values forward, in the work of Dean Spade and Merle Woo, who call for an intersectional politics of solidarity, multi-issue movement organizing, and revolution.[13]

One need not look to the 1970s for examples of working-class feminist movements for class and gender liberation. In two examples from 2018, the #MeToo movement and Spain's feminist general strike, the women's movement has taken on an intersectional character. In 2017 and 2018, after a number of celebrity actresses shared experiences of sexual assault by powerful men, a flood of women came forward with similar accounts from virtually every industry, saying "Me Too" to accounts of sexual harassment, exploitation, and gender violence. As journalist Sarah Lazare explained, these forms of sexual assault and harassment were not possible without the structures of power and exploitation made available to employers through workplace domination over workers. Most of these women were employed by, or dependent for work on, the men who assaulted them. The visibility of the A-list actors highlighted that working-class women, in hotel work, farm work, and factories, face sexual violence from employers and co-workers regularly. A 2017 letter from an organization of women farmworkers wrote that "even though we work in very different environments, we share a common experience of being preyed upon by individuals who have the power to hire, fire, blacklist and otherwise threaten our economic, physical, and emotional security." Class power and class dynamics contribute to men's ability to exploit women sexually as well as economically, and working-class feminist movements of resistance recognize these intersections.[14]

In another example, in Spain on March 8, 2019, International Working Women's Day, hundreds of thousands of women staged a one-day strike to end capitalism and for the liberation of women. Building off the #YoTeCreo ("I believe you") movement, women refused their paid work, as well as their unpaid work in the home and in kin networks, with a massive national strike. Spanish women demanded a change in unequal pay rates, sexual harassment, the gender division of labor, and women's "double day," in which women work at a paid job and are expected to do domestic labor when they return home. A big reason for the strike was to protest domestic violence and sexual abuse, as the actions were sparked by a gang rape following a bullfight in Pamplona. Again, collective action, collective interests, and power were reflected in the intersectional struggle with the slogan, "If we stop, the world stops." The power of this movement was born from the recognition of patriarchy as an intersectional phenomenon and the role of labor in providing leverage to challenge it.[15]

Also important in this regard are the feminist movements of Chile and Argentina in the 2010s. Here violence against women, especially immigrant women, and state bans on important health-care services such as abortion were leading causes for national demonstrations and strikes. Immigrant women, mostly Black, were subject to disproportionate violence because they faced more vulnerable and precarious social position as immigrants; as Black workers, they also faced a high degree of anti-Black racism in Chilean and Argentine society. The slogan that emerged in Argentina challenging femicide, "#NiUnaMenos" ("Not One More"), took hold too in Chile, where massive mobilizations in 2016 and 2017 led to larger and larger organizing efforts and protests. By 2019, the feminist movement prepared for a national strike on the 8th of March, the 8M movement, in which women built a national coordinated strike much like in Spain.[16]

The strength of the movement came from its intersectional nature, directly taking on state power and policy through the leverage of women's labor on the job and at home. There was also an explicit recognition of intersectional factors in shaping the movement. For example, feminist organizers used a class-based "sectoral" strategy in which different segments of the working class—workers, students, and neighborhood or rural communities—are brought together through intersectional organizing and mobilizing. The basic theory of the movement's sectoral strategy is that working-class people are engaged in different "sectors" of struggle—for example, housing, workplace struggles, against prisons, and so on. Feminist and anti-capitalist movements that bring these different actors in struggle together build working-class power across difference by addressing and taking up specific sectoral issues. It is an insightful strategy in that we can think of sectoral organizing as bringing different sectors of the working class into movements that address an array of class issues contingent on race, gender, ability, social position, et cetera.[17]

In the Chilean feminist movement, we see a brilliant example of intersectional class struggle in practice, one with transformative potential. According to movement participant Bree Busk, "contemporary Chilean feminism is refreshingly experimental and resilient . . . By maintaining a class struggle orientation and infusing their analysis with lessons learned from Black and Indigenous feminisms, this generation of feminists has advanced the struggle much farther than was previously considered possible." These mobilizations were the immediate precursors to the national uprisings in Chile in November 2019, which initiated a process to remove the constitution of the Pinochet dictatorship. The uprising was started mainly by teenage women with experience from feminist movements who began raucous protests against transit fare increases. It was these protests that launched the neighborhood assembly networks of class organizing that threatened to topple the government and rewrite the constitution and is still unfolding at this writing.[18]

Building Popular Power

The examples from the CIO, the Stonewall Riot, and Chile and Argentina all involve building popular power. Building popular power is a social movement practice of developing autonomous, democratic, and class-rooted organizations that can challenge the concentrated power of the state, capital, and the forms of social oppression and hierarchy that we experience. This means overcoming the atomization that leaves us disempowered and building combative organizations based in collective struggle and collective interests to fight on a variety of issues.[19]

We argue that key to building popular power is using workplace power and direct action tactics. As we've seen, a central dynamic of class—the relationship between labor and property—is an important aspect of power that working-class peoples can leverage to win fights against white supremacy and patriarchy. In political struggles, such as those of the Arab Spring in particular, workplace power became a source of strength from which social movements leveraged transformative change. We can see this in political struggles in the United States over immigration, education, taxes, and other government policy. In each of these cases, class analysis and workplace power help movements win meaningful victories and better fight against the array of forces leveled against us. This is true in movements combating climate change as well, in which an analysis of capitalism and the anti-capitalist practices of strikes and sectoral organizing are at the cutting edge of the current global climate movement. Building popular power means creating organizations that are accountable to working-class people and that can be leveraged to counter the institutions of the state, capitalism, white supremacy, and patriarchy.

Perhaps the most significant recent example of building popular power comes from the Arab Spring in Tunisia and Egypt. In those struggles—particularly the Egyptian people's movement to overthrow the Hosni Mubarak regime—workplace power, the power of labor, was the crucial leverage that popular movements used to force the end of the government. In both instances, people were suffering under authoritarian states backed by the United States. The demands of the movements included democratic reforms and improved economic conditions. In both Egypt and Tunisia, labor organizing determined the course of the struggle, providing the ultimate source of power to win against impossible odds.

In Tunisia, workers' struggles in the phosphate industry, and against the corrupt unions that were aligned with the regime, preceded the uprising of December of 2010. Jobs and economic reforms were the leading factors in those struggles, and these class conflicts initiated the revolt. With no economic prospects for work and facing harassment and criminalization from the regime, street vendor Mohamed Bouazizi lit himself on fire in front of the Tunis municipal offices. It was his act of self-immolation that sparked the Arab Spring. One of the central slogans in the Tunisian uprising—"A job is a right, you pack of thieves!"—reflected the class character of the struggle. One month later, after a wave of strikes and protests, many of which were in opposition to union leadership, the Tunisian dictator, Ben Ali, fled to Saudi Arabia. According to a leading scholar on the topic, Joel Beinin, it was the workers' strike in the capital of Tunis on January 14, 2011, that finally forced Ali from power. In Tunis, we see that mass uprising can raise pressure, but only the organized power of workers taking action on the job can force change. And it was workplace power—class power on the job, the strike—that led to the eventual victory in Tunisia.[20]

A similar story can be told in Egypt, where in 2011 a popular uprising against the Mubarak regime occupied a Cairo central plaza, Tahrir Square, but did not have the power to topple the regime. When the major Egyptian union federation sided with the government, the workers of Egypt forced a national strike on their own with tens of thousands of workers stopping production in strategic industries such as the Suez Canal Authority, the textile-producing factory Ghazl al-Mahalla, public transport in Cairo and Alexandra, and the national telecom services, Telecom Egypt. With the economy shut down through workplace action, Mubarak faced increasing pressure to end the standoff and get the country moving again by resigning. According to nongovernmental organizations on the ground, these strikes were "one of the most important factors leading to the rapidity of . . . Mubarak's decision to leave."[21]

Class dynamics permeated and defined the Arab Spring, and class power and the strategic use of workplace action combined with mass action were the definitive factors in the rise and initial victories of the social movement. According to Beinin, "class is, therefore, a key category for understanding both the social movements of workers and the unemployed" and the social distance between workers and the intelligentsia who claimed leadership of the uprisings. But workplace power is also key. In both Tunisia and Egypt, it was the power of labor to shut down the economy that won political victories for social movements.[22]

Much like Egypt and Tunisia, the immigrants' rights movement in the United States demonstrates that, for policy and political questions, working-class people's best leverage is in building popular power through disruptive struggle outside of official channels. In 2006 in the United States, millions of people took to the streets to protest planned legislation that would criminalize undocumented immigrants. The May Day immigration actions are considered by some to be the largest strike in the United States so far in the twenty-first century. Really more of a mass mobilization than a traditional strike, the 2006 demonstrations involved workers using direct action to influence state and party politics. Ultimately, they were successful—they stopped the law from moving forward and raised the issue of undocumented workers to a national platform.

The 2006 strike/mobilization was the precursor to a growing and increasingly powerful immigrants' rights movement. A few years later, young Latinx working-class activists occupied campaign offices of Barack Obama during his 2012 reelection campaign, contributing to the passage of the Deferred Action for Childhood Arrivals (DACA) law later that year. These were forerunners of the 2017 national "day without an immigrant" action, a mass direct action to further the class interests on immigration reform. The immigrants' rights movements of the last decade demonstrate the practice of building popular power through mass mobilizations and demonstrations, direct action, and not relying on politicians or the operation of the law to win the needed reforms.[23]

Political change is possible at a national level when movements take class politics seriously and use them as part of a strategy to build popular power. In Egypt, Tunisia, and with immigration reform in the United States, movements had an impact on national politics for the better, in some instances leading to the collapse of authoritarian governments and the beginning of new chapters of history. That type of change is also possible at a local level when workplace power is combined with a political agenda of intersectional class struggle. We can see examples of this recently in the efforts of the Chicago Teachers Union (CTU). In Chicago, one of the largest and wealthiest cities in the United States, schools are being cut and closed and teachers attacked and fired while the city says it has no money for education. Fed up with municipal claims to be penniless, the CTU took offensive action, striking for one day in 2016 for a corporate head tax and income tax on the city's highest earners. They followed up that action with a 2019 strike action for affordable housing. Teachers were condemned by the Democratic Party leadership of the city for this demand, but they pointed out that 17,000 of their students were homeless and that housing and other community needs were a core part of their work environment. Building from a place of power—their workplace—the teachers were able to create momentum around broader intersectional demands of the class.[24]

In another example, the struggle against climate change is also part of the class struggle. The growing climate justice movement demonstrates its intersectional nature, with Indigenous peoples, workers, students, and environmentalists pushing back and halting fossil fuel infrastructure projects. Different sectors of the class are taking action in different ways, as in the movement against the Dakota Access Pipeline, the #ShellNo campaign of "kayak-tivists" in 2015, the Unist'ot'en Camp, the European student strikes, and the fights against the Trans Mountain Pipeline project in British Columbia in 2019. In the student strikes of European secondary schools, for example, one sector of the class (students) employed militant and far-sighted strike tactics to pressure governments to change climate policy. Another example is Indigenous people in the Pacific Northwest and the North who are blocking pipeline construction and oil infrastructure projects. The synthesis of Indigenous struggles, climate, and capital projects show the interaction of capitalism, colonialism, and white supremacy. All these examples demonstrate intersectional class struggle in practice, bringing together factors of race, indigeneity, class, climate, and others in projects focused on building popular, class power.[25]

The Environmental Unionist Caucus, an ongoing organizing and education project of the Industrial Workers of the World (IWW), articulates these ideas. They write that "class struggle and the environment are issues which share common causes and need common solutions." For this, they look to the legacy of Judi Bari, a union and environmental activist from Northern California who sought to protect both old growth forests and jobs. Bari argued that the same companies that exploit and pollute the natural environment exploit and abuse workers, neglecting safety protections and paying them less and less. By linking struggles, Bari hoped to target the corporations and capital, and build solidarity between working people, environmentalists, and loggers. In 1990, she helped organize a "Redwood Summer," modeled on the civil rights movement, to bring people together and stop deforestation with direct action. For her activism, Bari was the target of an assassination attempt, a car bomb that nearly killed her. Nonetheless, her model of mass, class-based environmental organizing is a lasting legacy for today's movements. Her intersectional movement work, "green unionism," and Indigenous land struggles are leading the fight against climate change today.[26]

Bari's model of intersectional class-based organizing in environmental struggles is finding wide support and popularity in our own era of rapid climate change. If ever there were an issue to highlight the short-sighted, rapacious, and destructive power of capitalism's profit motive, it is the potentially devastating impact climate change will bring in the near future. Canadian author and activist Naomi Klein, in her book *This Changes Everything*, argues that the climate struggle is inseparable from the class struggle—that the same profit motive that exploits workers also exploits and destroys our natural world. Klein has said that, under capitalism, our "economic system is at war with many forms of life on earth" and that the class struggle for climate sustainability is part of the "unfinished business of liberation." It is more important than ever for our collective liberation and for our very survival that our struggle against capitalism and climate change is rooted in intersectional class struggle and building popular power.[27]

Workers' Democracy

Building organs of popular power is a way that we can change the world for the better and a key element of a bigger revolutionary strategy to transform society. In this broader transformative vision, workers' democracy and dual power emerge as two important parts of a strategy to build movements of popular power. Most of the breakthrough revolutions of history—the Paris Commune, the Spanish Revolution, and the Russian Revolution—were formed using these tools and in response to an intersection of social factors. In each of these struggles, different sectors of the class—workers in the workplace, neighbors in territorial assemblies, students, soldiers fighting militarism, or women in revolt—took organized action independently and collectively to reassert control over their lives and their governments. Often this was accomplished through creating new organs of democratic decision-making in federated workplace, neighborhood, women's, and other organizations.

A situation of dual power emerges when the organs of popular working-class democracy are powerful enough to vie for control with bourgeois governments. From this vantage, with the right strategy and some luck, it is possible to erode the power of the state, capital, and forms of social oppression and to begin to create something new in their place. Creating the conditions of popular power can not only challenge oppressive power but also limit and potentially end the systems that oppress us by replacing them with democratic working-class organizations.

One of the bridges between struggles for reform and those of social transformation is the general strike. The general strike is the organized collective refusal to work on the part of a majority of workers in any given industry, sector, city, or region. Its power is that it disrupts the entire economy and demonstrates that it is the workers, not the owners, who ultimately make society run. The strike could be based in the workplace, be a popular uprising against war, come from women demanding improved social conditions, or come from defiant students in rebellion, but it must ultimately draw in workplace struggle to shut down the economy. From the foundation of a general strike, workers can transform that refusal into outright control of our lives by creating directly democratic organizations. The power to withhold labor and force a crisis on ruling interests or demand new progressive gains is also the power to create something new, to reclaim power and make it more democratic, horizontal, and transparent. In fact, very quickly, movements that grow up in opposition to oppression, if they become powerful enough, can move to a transformative, revolutionary footing that can build new, directly democratic institutions and social relationships.

Take, for instance, the origins of the International Longshore and Warehouse Union (ILWU), one of the strongest and most class-conscious unions in the United States today. Dockworkers in San Francisco the 1930s faced horrible and dangerous working conditions. Their jobs were precarious, they were hired by the day with no guarantee of employment, and workplace safety did not exist. Workers were routinely killed or maimed under falling cargo. Fed up with these conditions, workers wanted a degree of control over their workplace, union recognition, and, importantly for the practice of precarious employment, the ability to choose who would work on the docks. In 1934, the employers refused this demand, which they correctly viewed as a curtailment of their power, and forced a strike. As usual, the employers relied on violence to break the strike—police killed two striking workers and the National Guard was called in to get the ports running for commerce once again. Very quickly, the funeral procession for the slain workers became a general strike, one that brought thousands of workers into the streets. So many workers walked off the job that the procession stretched a mile and half down San Francisco's Market Street. The strike expanded along the West Coast and affected all Pacific commerce that relied on the docks. With this, shipping employers faced pressure from other businesses and the federal government to settle the strike. And they did. After just four days of the general strike and West Coast port shutdown, the employers asked for arbitration. The outcome, following a very long process of negotiation, was that the workers won all their major demands, including union hiring halls. The longshore general strike saw workers seizing their workplaces along the docks of the West Coast and reasserting control of their labor. From there, it's a short step to outright control of an important hub of distribution, and from there, the whole economy.[28]

Whereas longshore workers used the power of their labor, other struggles demonstrate that there are a variety of paths toward working-class democracy. For example, Parisian workers deployed new democratic structures in their neighborhoods developed during the 1871 Paris Commune. Sparked by a conflict between the governments of Prussia and France that led to war, the city of Paris was abandoned by the French government during a Prussian siege. In that absence, workers took control of the city's means of defense and set up some of the farthest-reaching democratic and revolutionary structures of governance in the modern period. Key among them was the practice of direct, rather than representative, democracy. The Paris workers erected a federated structure of governance, whereby assemblies in the city's *arrondissements* (neighborhoods) held ultimate decision-making power, placing the greatest authority at the bottom of government rather than the top. The *arrondissements* elected delegates to a citywide executive municipal council tasked with implementing the decisions of the city's workers. These were delegates, tasked with specific activities and subject to instant recall if they strayed from the democratic mandates; they were not representatives, who have the power to represent the general will of the electorate. The democratic structures of the Paris Commune survived for 70 days until they were undone in the ruthless suppression by the bourgeois Aldophe Thiers government, a bloodbath that saw tens of thousands of Parisian workers and revolutionists killed.[29]

Like Paris, German workers also used the crisis of war to construct a worker-run society. In this instance, war industry workers, soldiers, went on strike directly to end World War I. For many on the left during the war, a workers' and soldiers' strike was the only way to stop the carnage. Indeed, in the United States, socialist and feminist Hellen Keller argued that U.S. involvement in the war was not meant to defend the country and spread democracy, as politicians and capitalists claimed. "Congress is not preparing to defend the people of the United States," she wrote; instead, "it is planning to protect the capital of American speculators and investors in Mexico, South America, China, and the Philippine Islands." Keller wanted workers and soldiers in the United States to strike to prevent U.S. involvement.[30]

That task fell to German workers, who, as parties to the war from the outset, had faced the worst of the atrocities. In October 1918, German sailors refused orders to prepare for an attack on the British Navy. When the conspirators were arrested, hundreds of other sailors met at the Union House in the German city of Kiel, and the mutiny turned into a rebellion. Sailors and workers demanded "Peace and Bread." Their demonstration to release the captive comrades was confronted with bullets, and the rebellion became a full-scale revolt, spreading throughout the ranks and helping to precipitate the end of the war. This was only possible because the mass soldiers' revolt turned into a revolutionary crisis in Germany, with soldiers and workers striking for a revolutionary transformation of German society. Indeed, the German Revolution of 1918, started by soldiers and continued by workers, ended the monarchy and brought about the creation of the Weimar Republic. It threatened a widespread workers' revolution along soviet lines had not the Socialist Party leadership quelled the revolution and assassinated leading revolutionaries. By organizing, and taking to revolt, working-class people can not only shift major government policy and end major wars but also radically transform society. [31]

World War I also ignited revolution in Russia. In this instance, it was a women's strike on International Working Women's Day in 1917 that sparked the peasants' revolt and general social uprising of workers that led to revolution. Women demonstrated against horrible living conditions produced by Russia's involvement in the war and demanded bread and domestic improvements. At the end of the day, 100,000 working women were in the streets. The next day, their numbers grew to 150,000, and the women's action spread to a general strike in St. Petersburg and other cities. As in Germany at the end of the war, the strike spread to different sectors of the class, encouraging soldiers to defect and refuse orders. Workers, peasants, and soldiers formed democratic soviets, popular decision-making bodies that became a source of "dual power," a separate form of democratic self-governance that was able to end Russia's involvement in the war and topple the tsarist autocracy. Unfortunately, this early form of workers' revolutionary democracy was usurped, and the most democratic and egalitarian measures were undone in the Bolshevik counterrevolution of 1918–1921. In Russia, for a short while at least, revolutionary struggles produced dual power by developing and combining the struggles of different sectors of the class.[32]

Anarchists called this process "building the seed of the new in the shell of the old." It played out in the Russian Revolution with the creation of the soviets, the Paris Commune in the democratic *arrondissements*, and the Spanish Revolution of 1936. In Spain, the model of syndicated and federated workers' organizations spread through workplaces and the countryside in the early twentieth century. These organizations contributed to a rent strike in Barcelona in 1931 and by 1936 had built a women's organization, *Mujeres Libres*, which had 80,000 members at the time of the revolution. When the Spanish colonial military staged a coup to topple the left-wing government in 1936, the workers were ready; using their preexisting organizations, they collectivized workplaces and neighborhoods. After a very short revolutionary uprising, workers immediately began to take over the mechanisms of business and to run them in their own interests. Barbershops, textile factories, streetcars, and even hotels and restaurants were run on an egalitarian, working-class basis. Many of them worked more efficiently than they had under capitalism. The transition was so complete that, on the day after the revolution, the head of the Catalan government, Luis Companys, met with the anarchist leadership of the workers' union, the Confederación Nacional del Trabajo (CNT), and confessed that he was powerless—that the workers had won. The anarchist leadership squandered this moment, however; instead of using the power of the workers to construct a new egalitarian society and smash the old bourgeois order, they allowed Companys and the republican government free reign, a mobility it was able to use to regroup and eventually crush the revolution.[33]

Whereas workers, women, and soldiers can foment revolution, students too can act as revolutionary class agents and build organs of direct democracy and dual power. One instance from the United States is the national student strikes against the bombing of Cambodia in 1970. These were the strikes that led to National Guard soldiers killing students at Kent State and other U.S. campuses. Virtually every campus in the United States was shut down during the strikes—four million students participated, and students at New York University hung a banner reading, "They Can't Kill Us All." Unfortunately, they were not able to bring any other sector of the working class into the strike.[34]

A more compelling example of student strikes turning into a revolutionary power might be the May 1968 uprisings in France, in which student revolts grew into a national general strike. A series of occupations against capitalism and imperialism by French students sparked sympathy strikes from radicalized French workers all over the country. At the height, eleven million workers participated, roughly 22 percent of the entire French population. Fearing revolution and civil war, French President Charles De Gaulle briefly fled to Germany. However, with concessions from the government, the revolutionary moment passed, and the movement fizzled. But the May 1968 uprisings demonstrate that the student sector in collective revolt can, in conjunction with other sectors of the class, build power in democratic organizations and threaten revolutionary change.[35]

Conclusion

More than a theory, the intersectional class-struggle tradition is developed from movement practice and helps provide an analysis that can improve our understanding, strategy, and tactics. Class is infused into all political questions and social issues, and the tools of class struggle show us a way out of the political morass in which we find ourselves during the first half of the twenty-first century. The intersectional class-struggle tradition contributes a power analysis in which the complex interrelation of social issues is considered part of a capitalist totality that needs to be struggled against holistically. Whereas profit is the prime motivator of the system, the place of profit generation—the workplace—is an important source of power for all working-class struggles, even those not directly tied to economic or job issues. Because social issues are intersectional, the class-struggle tradition has never been about narrowly defined workplace struggle and instead touches on a whole range of social questions and political topics, including militarism, immigration, citizenship, political legitimacy, and climate.

The sectoral approach explored here shows that various sectors of the class (workers, women, students, soldiers, or others) can lead a particular struggle, but to become revolutionary it is also important to bring multiple sectors of the class together in transformative movements. Here the class-struggle tradition contributes movement practice that can help further working-class interests in all their diversity. These include the workplace strike that takes action on the job, the mass strike that brings in diverse members of the class to fight in important struggles, direct action on and off the job, and political strikes that can change government policy or even entire governments. The most hopeful parts of this tradition, the general strike and building dual power, can in some instances transform society and create the possibility of collective liberation. When we think about contemporary questions of race, feminism, colonialism, the environment, and others, the intersectional class-struggle tradition brings us a long way closer to freedom.

Conclusion

On Hope and Solidity

All that is solid melts into air.

—Karl Marx

Writing about the capitalist revolution of the early nineteenth century and the transformations of material society and cultural values that came with it, Marx said that, with social revolutions as momentous as the rise of capitalism, "all that is solid melts into air, all that is sacred is profaned." When capitalist social relations took over from feudal society, with the pursuit of profit its sole animating force, old notions of family, chivalry, and deference were abandoned. Marx was trying to show the direction between material and cultural aspects of social change. Transformations of material relations changed people's consciousness and the very foundations of the old order. The social forms that people had come to accept, the beliefs that were a fundamental part of how society operated, suddenly were no more. The places of order and belonging were gone.

Marx's insights were revolutionary in themselves in the mid-nineteenth century, but they can only carry us so far in our study of class. Not just from material causes, the erosion of solidity in social relations can originate from changes in people's consciousness that affect the material world. E. P. Thompson's work shows us exactly this. He writes in the preface to *The Making of the English Working Class* that class is, in fact, an abstraction. He reminds us that, if we try to pin it down, "stop it in its tracks," look for a concrete material reality of class, we are left only with individuals, paychecks, and pink slips. Class resists this specificity because, as much as we can say it is inherent in the nature of social relationships, it is just as much about how people think about themselves, about culture and ideas, patterns of consciousness, habits, interests. These are all practices of the mind; indeed, one might go so far to say that social relationships are made meaningful only in so far as we consciously articulate them in thought. In this revised vision, class is both material and cultural, contingent on particular historical circumstances, and constantly changing and rearticulating itself given the array of social forces and ideas present in the world.

Ultimately, the emphasis on the intersection of material and cultural factors, and the constructedness of social structures, is about restoring human agency to the course of history. It is about building a politics of hope in fairly dark times. The minute we stop thinking wages are legitimate, reject white supremacy, or question housework, and start acting on those beliefs, then the very hard, material reality of social structure will begin to melt into air. At a time of terrifying climate change, mass deportations, police violence, wealth inequality, and global pandemics, we need an effective politics of transformative change, if only to rebuild our hope in the prospects for humankind. Intersectional class struggle is an important reminder to open up the terrain of social transformation and the possibility of greater human emancipation. It is a tradition that invites one to hope.

Given these tensions between materiality and culture, structure and agency, how to best answer Marx's unanswered question from 150 years ago: What, exactly, is class? Clearly there is no one, singular answer, as the definition of class is contingent on circumstances, culture, property relations, and ultimately how we decide to define it. But given the picture of class developed in this book, we can say that one important definition of class is a shared perspective or set of collective interests with no one, universal, or singular working-class politics. Instead, class is made up of a patchwork of intersecting and overlapping experiences, positions, ideas, and interests. What emerges from the patchwork is the politics of solidarity and mutual aid that makes up the intellectual tradition and working-class movement practice of intersectional class struggle; the idea introduced by Clarence Coe, that we are all in it together, all in the "same boat." Importantly, this includes opposition to wages and property in capitalism, and the fundamental structures of white supremacy and patriarchy embedded in those institutions. In this tradition, we can see that the working class is made up of all of us, in all our contradictions and complications. Class is made of ourselves.

There are a couple of core ideas we need to mind regarding these conclusions about class. If we take as our starting point the advent of capitalism to understand contemporary class politics, then relationships of property are at the foundation for the lived reality of class. Property ownership, a social structure of exclusive control, gives the owners of society tremendous power. This is especially true of profitable property—capital. The ones who are able to exploit people without property are those who derive wealth from real estate; productive machinery in factories; access to knowledge, skills, and markets; and ownership of information. Ownership and the split between wages and profits is what structures the "permanent antagonism" between working people and employers, the idea William Sylvis introduced in the nineteenth century. It is the animating force of much of contemporary politics and social affairs. Ownership remains the basic divide at the foundation of class to this day.

By the time social thinkers such as Proudhon and Marx arrived on the scene, the critique of wages, property, and profit became far more systematic. Property, rent, and wages were all part of a singular whole, a capitalist totality that alienated workers from our work, our labor, and our very selves. In addition, capital constructed social classes, opposing collective interests based on relationships to property. This structural understanding places class beyond definitions of income, education, or even employment. Instead, it shows that class is a position and set of ideas that extends from the social relations of property into every segment of society, including the unemployed, the homeless, and homemakers, all members of the working class by nature of their relationship to ownership and capital.

Lack of ownership means lack of control, and the relationship of property, profits, wages, and exploitation was therefore akin to slave labor. These systems were so similar that the abolitionist movement debated whether the abolition of wages should be included in the demands for the abolition of slavery, both as forms of labor exploitation. Although racialized chattel slavery was a category apart from the wage system, incomparably worse in most ways, in one aspect the comparison works. Both enslaved people and workers lost control of their labor on the job. They were not paid fully or at all for the value they created, and they had specific collective interests opposed to those of the ownership class. This systemic understanding of class shows us that class is a social relationship and that profits and wages are rooted in property and labor exploitation.

But the "material" conditions of wages and property are only one way to understand class. The other is through culture and consciousness. By the mid–twentieth century, writers such as Rudolf Rocker, Thompson, and Stuart Hall showed the ways in which class was socially and culturally constructed. For Thompson, the notion that class could be determined with scientific certainty, as many Marxists claimed, was wrong. Class, instead, was contingent on experience, reflection, consciousness, and culture. How workers thought about and acted on their circumstances was just as important as the "objective" conditions in which they operated. Thompson showed class to be a process—a process of critical consciousness and action—a process of class formation. Other thinkers such as Rocker and Hall demonstrated the complex interrelation of base and superstructure, showing that a singular determination of causality coming from the material base was faulty. Cultural and material factors shape and influence one another in particular historical "articulations," arrangements of forces and ideas that make social structure and cultural meaning possible in specific ways. One strength of the cultural emphasis is the focus on agency. If structure and culture are the result of human activity, they can be shaped and remade with concerted human effort. This understanding of class exposes the possibility of liberatory and transformative struggle for us all.

We can see the synthesis of material and cultural factors of class in the lived experiences of working people. In the words of Selma James, there need be no dichotomous tension between culture and materiality because people's experiences and identities are part and parcel of "the totality of their capitalist lives." She argues that culture cannot be restricted to a secondary role in social causality. She writes:

"To delimit culture is to reduce it to a decoration of daily life. Culture is plays and poetry about the exploited; ceasing to wear miniskirts and taking to trousers instead; the class between the should of Black Baptism and the guilt of white Protestantism. Culture is also the shrill of the alarm clock that rings at 6 a.m. when a Black woman in London wakes her children to get them ready for the baby-minder. Culture is how cold she feels at the bus stop and then how hot in the crowded bus. Culture is how you feel on Monday morning at eight when you clock in, wishing it was Friday, wishing your life away."[1]

These lived experiences, the foundation of identity, are, in the words of Selma James, "the very substance of class." Understanding the intersections of materiality and culture, class, race, and gender can help build the liberatory struggles and future we desperately need. Confronting the capitalist totality can help us get there.

With a foundation in culture and materiality, and with concepts such as "articulation" from Hall, we can see the intersectional nature of social oppression. If class is made from particular historical articulations, then race and gender are unquestionably structural and cultural factors that inform that articulation. The end of slavery was not just the end of the legal and economic forms of human ownership, but also meant the continuation of structures of white supremacy and racial hierarchy that influenced class formation through and beyond the twentieth century. The circumstance is similar with gender. The need to keep the costs of social reproduction down means that capital has a vested interest in patriarchal control of women's labor and bodies on and off the job. Thus, the end of feudal property relations did not spell the end for the system of patriarchy that undergirded the old order. Instead, the strength of patriarchy was redoubled with the advent of capitalism, and it won't go away until we address the systems of exploitation present in the capitalist "social factory."

This gives us a much more complicated picture of the capitalist totality. The totality is not just about work done on the job, about the forms of profit accumulation, but also about the forms of white supremacy and patriarchy inherent and embedded in the structures of capitalism. As Silvia Federici says, "Capitalism, as a social-economic system, is necessarily committed to racism and sexism." This necessity comes from structural factors of capital, the dehumanization necessary for exploitation, the competition of labor markets that foster

racial antagonism, the unremunerated forms of labor in social reproduction, and the gender division of labor. Capitalism can only function "by denigrating the 'nature' of those it exploits," Federici writes,
of "women, colonial subjects, the descendants of African slaves, the
immigrants displaced by globalization."[2] This totality is our modern
problem. It remains the basis of our contemporary struggles.

One key insight that came from the social movements in the 1960s
and 1970s, particularly from Black feminist thought, was the emphasis on difference and diversity within claims to social equality and
liberty. Indeed, this is a core insight for our understanding of class,
in that, even though we share similar structural conditions of class,
we are affected differently. Race, gender, sexuality, disability, immigration status, and other factors all inform our class position and
our interests. Even though it makes sense to continue to talk about a
working class as those who lack access to profitable property, there
is no uniform, singular class interest to shape political struggle in
the present period. Instead, the politics of class are diffuse, multiple,
contingent, and qualified. This does not mean the end of class as an
analytic, or the end of the history of the working class, but a more
nuanced, accurate, and ultimately liberatory vision of class politics to
guide our political struggles in the here and now.

Because of this, for example, working-class intellectuals Selma
James and Mariarosa Dalla Costa regard the movement for Black
liberation associated with civil rights in the United States as a class
struggle. Because African Americans largely occupied the bottom rung
of the American working class, their struggle for liberation and inte-
gration necessarily addressed the concerns of the class, and therefore
were not a diversion from class struggle but a fundamental component of that struggle. Borrowing ideas from C. L. R. James, they write
that "the demands of Black people and the forms of struggle created
by Black people were the most comprehensive *working-class* demands
and the most advanced *working-class* struggle."[3] Selma James goes on
to say that "it is not then that the Black movement 'wandered off into
the class struggle' . . . it *was* the class struggle." In a more contemporary example, queer and trans movements speak to this diversity
of class struggle. Because LGBTQ+ peoples are working people, are
racialized and gendered in particular ways, and experience distinct
forms of capitalist articulation that are enacted against them and from

which they rebel, they too are part of the working class and intersectional class struggle. "Our experiences and oppressions as women, as queers, as folks with disabilities," writes movement organizer JOMO, "cannot be separated from the capitalist structure of society." Indeed, Black feminism highlights the heterogeneity of social definitions such as "women." This concept of difference extends to "class" as well. [4]

With this more informed understanding of class, we can see the practice of intersectional class struggle emerge in broad outline. The nature of working-class struggle has always been in and outside the workplace. Issues of rent, civil rights, gender oppression, political reforms, and others have all been part of class struggle. Emphasizing structure and power, the intersectional class-struggle tradition highlights the importance of direct action taken by working-class people. The most potent form of direct action is in the workplace strike. By striking at the core site of profit accumulation, workplace actions hit the capitalist class in the primary motivator for capitalism. In the words of anarchist revolutionary Warlaam Tcherkesoff, "the power of the ruling class is based on the wealth produced by the people" on the job. Therefore, "to free themselves from this domination, the people must refuse to yield up the fruit of their toil to their masters" at the very site of exploitation through strikes and collective organization. [5]

For social movements outside of the workplace, this source of power can be extremely influential, determinative, on the ability to win. If we scale up from the workplace strike to mass direct action, political strikes, and general strikes, we can see how intersectional class struggle has the power to change not only our immediate circumstances but the possibility to create a radical transformation of society toward greater freedom and justice. Again, in the words of Tcherkesoff, "It is not by a political, but by an economic struggle; not ballot-boxes, but by strikes; not by a decision of parliament, but by a well organized and triumphant general strike that the people can inaugurate a new era." When workers develop dual power, the mechanisms of self-governance to rival that of capitalists, the potential for revolutionary struggle emerges. This analysis and transformative vision lie at the heart of intersectional class struggle.[6]

But social struggle is not so easy, and here we are left with some significant challenges. The major questions before the intersectional class-struggle tradition are the issue of state power and the institutionalization of forms of resistance, particularly in legalized unions. State violence is a major repressive force against social movements, and mitigating or deflecting the use of that violence is a core concern for class struggle. Therefore, how to relate to the state is a major question, whether to avoid and ignore it, enter and redirect it, or something else altogether are all strategies with serious pitfalls and problems. Another major question is how to organize and institutionalize the forms of resistance that have the force to topple property without recapitulating popular power into the structures of authoritarianism, capitalism, and oppression. History demonstrates that unions and other forms of organizational resistance once institutionalized and accepted by the state tend to pacify rather than amplify resistance. Yet without these forms, movement victories are ephemeral in a system with a relentless pursuit of profit and exploitation.[7]

Given this picture, what is to be done? One answer to this question came one hundred years before this writing, in the work of Vladimir Ilyich Lenin, who was attempting to build a revolutionary movement of European workers. His vision was that workers would forever have trouble articulating revolutionary working-class politics, and that a vanguard party was necessary to shepherd in a revolutionary break with capitalism. But this work argues otherwise. Given the picture of class formation here, of multiple and diverse interests and perspectives, there can be no singular set of interests of "the" working class. The class struggle is ever-present and varied. It has no fixed point of struggle, and instead is rooted in the multivariate experiences of all our lives, all of us who compose the working class. For Selma James and others, this meant that there could be no singular vanguard. James correctly argues, "Since the Leninist model assumes a vanguard expressing the total class interests, it bears no relation to the reality we have been describing, where no one section of the class can express the experience and interest of, and pursue the struggle for, any other section."[8]

Instead, our movements need a collective composition that reflects and respects this diversity. Movements grown from solidarity, mutual respect, and understanding are powerful indeed. It is possible to make claims to collective and cooperative human emancipation based on difference and contingency. Plainly, concepts such as difference are core to the practice of liberty and social freedom, which ring hollow if restricted and limited to particularist definitions. It is only in this manner, through collective struggle and collective power, that we can hope to change the entrenched structures of violence that contribute to exploitation and planetary decline. This is more than a theoretical question of the limits of structure and the possibility of human agency; it is a practical question about where we can go from here.

Thankfully, difficult theoretical questions can, at times, have surprising practical answers. Often we can learn about the nature of power and struggle, structure and agency, from those who have come before, from the voices of workers, enslaved peoples, and sectors of the oppressed. For example, Harriet Jacobs's *Narrative of the Life of a Slave Girl* is a powerful testament to human agency and perseverance against the most inhumane of social structures. In her strategies to defend herself from her owner's sexual violence, she remarked on the difficult but ultimately hopeful relationship between structure and agency: "My master had power and law on his side," she wrote, "I had a determined will. There is might in each." Although the power arrayed against us is daunting, for Jacobs and innumerable other voices in the intersectional class-struggle tradition, we find that, in our will, in our self-definition, in our resistance, we are truly mighty.[9]

Reflection, thought, will, agency, and action. These are the ingredients for successful struggle. With new understandings of structure and culture, we can open up the limits of the possible. The hard structural boundaries that we think a fixed part of our material reality are as much social constructions as anything else. On inspection, they break down as fluid and fungible, in some circumstances to be completely undone and replaced with something new. With this understanding, new horizons of human emancipation and achievement become possible. We don't have to settle for what our imaginations can conceive. We can continually struggle against the structural components of our society and the cultural limits of our imaginations. In the act of struggle, all becomes possible. The material and cultural are not so fixed and immutable. Slavery was ended by slaves, capitalism will die too, and a new era of human emancipation will be born. All that was once seen as solid will melt into air.

Notes

Preface

1. Nate Cohn, "Why Trump Won: Working-Class Whites," *New York Times*, November 9, 2016, https://www.nytimes.com/2016/11/10/upshot/why-trump-won-working-class-whites.html; Nia-Malika Henderson, "Race and Racism in the 2016 Campaign," CNN, August 31, 2016, https://www.cnn.com/2016/08/31/politics/2016-election-donald-trump-hillary-clinton-race/index.html; Charlotte Alter, "How Trump Turned 2016 into a Referendum on Gender," October 8, 2016, *TIME*, https://time.com/4523900/donald-trump-gender; Domenico Montanaro, "7 Reasons Donald Trump Won The Presidential Election," NPR, November 12, 2016, https://www.npr.org/2016/11/12/501848636/7-reasons-donald-trump-won-the-presidential-election.

2. Michèle Lamont, Bo Yun Park, and Elena Ayala-Hurtado, "Trump's Electoral Speeches and His Appeal to the American White Working Class," *British Journal of Sociology* 68, Suppl. 1 (November 2017): S153–180; Donald Trump, "Remarks at the Summit Sports and Ice Complex in Dimondale, Michigan | The American Presidency Project," https://www-presidency-ucsb-edu.offcampus.lib.washington.edu/documents/remarks-the-summit-sports-and-ice-complex-dimondale-michigan; Pew Research Center, "An Examination of the 2016 Electorate, Based on Validated Voters: For Most Trump Voters, 'Very Warm' Feelings for Him Endured," August 9, 2018, https://www.pewresearch.org/politics/2018/08/09/an-examination-of-the-2016-electorate-based-on-validated-voters.

3. Pew Research Center, "An Examination of the 2016 Electorate"; Matthew Yglesias, "What Really Happened in 2016, in 7 Charts," *Vox*, September 18, 2017, https://www.vox.com/policy-and-politics/2017/9/18/16305486/what-really-happened-in-2016; Keeanga-Yamahtta Taylor, "Black Feminism and the Combahee River Collective," *Monthly Review*, January 1, 2019, https://monthlyreview.org/2019/01/01/black-feminism-and-the-combahee-river-collective.

4. Jim Tankersley, "How Trump Won: The Revenge of Working-Class Whites," *Washington Post*, https://www.washingtonpost.com/news/wonk/wp/2016/11/09/how-trump-won-the-revenge-of-working-class-whites; Nate Silver, "The Mythology of Trump's 'Working Class' Support," FiveThirtyEight .com, May 3, 2016, https://fivethirtyeight.com/features/the-mythology-of -trumps-working-class-support; Cohn, "Why Trump Won"; Sally Kohn, "Nothing Donald Trump Says on Immigration Holds Up," *TIME*, June 29, 2016, https://time.com/4386240/donald-trump-immigration-arguments.

5. Adam Harris, "Bernie Sanders Reached Out to Black Voters. Why Didn't It Work?," *Atlantic*, March 10, 2020, https://www.theatlantic.com/politics /archive/2020/03/bernie-sanders-black-voters/607789; Meagan Day, "Bernie Sanders Should Embrace the Demand to Defund the Police," *Jacobin*, June 10, 2020, https://jacobinmag.com/2020/06/bernie-sanders-defund-police-uprising. Bernie's position opposing police abolition and supporting increased police funding, representing the extreme left of the Democratic Party, became the position of the Joe Biden campaign in their "unity platform" during the general election. *WSJ* Noted, "Here's Where the Democrats Stand on Police Funding, Marijuana and Medicare," *Wall Street Journal*, July 29, 2020, https://www.wsj.com/articles/heres-where-the-democrats-stand-on-police -funding-marijuana-and-medicare-11596052231; "Biden, Sanders Release Progressive Unity Platform for Democratic Party," *US News & World Report*, July 8, 2020, https://www.usnews.com/news/elections/articles/2020-07-08/ biden-sanders-release-progressive-unity-platform-for-democratic-party.

6. Dominic Rushe, "Coronavirus Has Widened America's Vast Racial Wealth Gap, Study Finds," *Guardian*, June 19, 2020, https://www.theguardian .com/us-news/2020/jun/19/coronavirus-pandemic-billioinaires-racial -wealth-gap; Dedrick Asante-Muhammad, Chuck Collins, and Omar Ocampo, "White Supremacy Is the Preexisting Condition: Eight Solutions to Ensure Economic Recovery Reduces the Racial Wealth Divide," June 19, 2020, IPS, https: //ips-dc.org/white-supremacy-preexisting-condition-eight-solutions-economic -recovery-racial-wealth-divide/; Bureau of Labor Statistics, "Labor Force Statistics from the Current Population Survey: E-16. Unemployment Rates by Age, Sex, Race, and Hispanic or Latino Ethnicity," https://www.bls.gov/web/ empsit/cpsee_e16.htm. Jonnelle Marte, "Gap in U.S. Black and White Unemployment Rates Is Widest in Five Years," *Reuters*, July 2, 2020, https://www .reuters.com/article/us-usa-economy-unemployment-race-idUSKBN2431X7; Tom Huddleston Jr., "Jeff Bezos Added $13 Billion to His Net Worth in One Day—and That's a Record," CNBC, July 21, 2020, https://www.cnbc.com /2020/07/21/bezos-record-multibillion-dollar-net-worth-gain-bloomberg .html; Ezra Kaplan and Jo Ling Kent, "Eighth Amazon Warehouse Worker Dies from COVID-19," NBC News, May 21, 2020, https://www.nbcnews.com/ news/us-news/eighth-amazon-warehouse-worker-dies-covid-19-n1212546; CBS News, "Amazon Employee Who Advocated for Warehouse Workers

Says She Was Fired in 'a 30-Second Phone Call,'" CBS News, May 13, 2020, https://www.cbsnews.com/news/amazon-worker-fired-coronavirus-maren -costa-emily-cunningham; Dave Lee, "Amazon Doubles Quarterly Profit despite Covid-19 Costs," *Financial Times*, July 30, 2020, https://www.ft.com/ content/7a42b1d8-9ca7-4827-aaae-729fdb7637f5.

7. Sarah Jones, "Essential Workers Are Still Dying From Coronavirus," *Intelligencer*, June 26, 2020, https://nymag.com/intelligencer/2020/06/essential -workers-are-still-dying-from-coronavirus.html; Les Leopold, "COVID-19's Class War," *American Prospect*, July 28, 2020, https://prospect.org/api/content /279de642-d055-11ea-a02c-1244d5f7c7c6. Tiffany N. Ford, Sarah Reber, and Richard V. Reeves, "Race Gaps in COVID-19 Deaths Are Even Bigger than They Appear," June 16, 2020, https://www.brookings.edu/blog/up-front/2020 /06/16/race-gaps-in-covid-19-deaths-are-even-bigger-than-they-appear; Harvard T.H. Chan School of Public Health, "Health Disparities between Blacks and Whites Run Deep," https://www.hsph.harvard.edu/news/hsph-in-the-news/ health-disparities-between-blacks-and-whites-run-deep; Elise Gould and Valerie Wilson, "Black Workers Face Two of the Most Lethal Preexisting Conditions for Coronavirus—Racism and Economic Inequality," June 1, 2020, https://www.epi.org/publication/black-workers-covid; Juliana Menasce Horowitz, "Views on Why Black Americans Face Higher COVID-19 Hospitalization Rates Vary by Party, Race and Ethnicity," June 26, 2020, https://www .pewresearch.org/fact-tank/2020/06/26/views-on-why-black-americans -face-higher-covid-19-hospitalization-rates-vary-by-party-race-and-ethnicity.

8. George C. Comninel, "Marx and the Politics of the First International," *Journal of the Research Group on Socialism and Democracy Online*, July 19, 2015, http://sdonline.org/65/marx-and-the-politics-of-the-first-international; Karl Marx, *The Communist Manifesto* (New York: W.W. Norton, 2012). Wolfgang Eckhardt, *The First Socialist Schism: Bakunin vs. Marx in the International Working Men's Association* (Oakland: PM Press, 2016).

9. David R. Roediger, *Seizing Freedom: Slave Emancipation and Liberty for All* (Brooklyn: Verso, 2014), 110–119. National liberation struggles, in particular Byron's experience in Greece, were likely his leading inspiration. Jared Hickman, *Byronic Abolitionism* (Oxford: Oxford University Press, 2016); Jake C. Spangler, "Intertextual Abolitionists: Frederick Douglass, Lord Byron, and the Print, Politics, and Language of Slavery," MA thesis, DePaul University, 2019.

Introduction

1. Michael Keith Honey, *Black Workers Remember: An Oral History of Segregation, Unionism, and the Freedom Struggle* (Berkeley: University of California Press, 2002), 360. Ellipses in original.

2. Honey, *Black Workers Remember*, 45–46, 73–75.

3. Honey, *Black Workers Remember*, 362. Following Patricia Hill Collins in her work *Black Feminist Thought*, we will use the word "we" in reference to the authorship and interventions of this book. Collins expresses this most eloquently when she argues that she fundamentally identifies with the tradition she delineates, and reflects that the knowledge produced in her work is part of an historical and collective process of which she is a small part. When appropriate, we follow the same practice here. Patricia Hill Collins, *Black Feminist Thought: Knowledge, Consciousness, and the Politics of Empowerment* (New York: Routledge, 2008), 22.

4. André Gorz, *Farewell to the Working Class* (Boston: South End Press, 1982).

5. Guy Standing, *The Precariat: The New Dangerous Class* (London: Bloomsbury Academic, 2016); Michael Hardt and Antonio Negri, *Multitude: War and Democracy in the Age of Empire* (New York: Penguin Books, 2005).

6. Kim Moody, *On New Terrain: How Capital Is Reshaping the Battleground of Class War* (Chicago: Haymarket Books, 2017); Linda Yueh, "Are We Living in the Second Gilded Age?," BBC News, May 15, 2014, https://www.bbc.com/news/business-27419853; Thomas Piketty, *Capital in the Twenty-First Century*, trans. Arthur Goldhammer (Cambridge, Massachusetts: Belknap Press, 2017).

7. Melvin Leiman, *The Political Economy of Racism* (Chicago: Haymarket Books, 2010), 8, 313.

8. G.A. Cohen, *Karl Marx's Theory of History* (Princeton, New Jersey: Princeton University Press, 2000), 77. Vivek Chibber, "Rescuing Class From the Cultural Turn," *Catalyst: A Journal of Theory and Strategy* 1, no. 1 (Spring 2017), https://catalyst-journal.com/vol1/no1/cultural-turn-vivek-chibber. We find Chibber's definition—"Class is defined by agents' objective location within a social structure, which in turn generate a set of interests that govern those agents' social action"—to not be that helpful. Working-class social agents define their interests along a whole spectrum of structural positions, of which class is one but race and gender are others. Nevertheless, their cultural values around conflict, aspirational hopes, or other qualities might foster other types of articulations. Indeed, his work sets up a dichotomous view of "material" and "cultural" explanations of class that this work is trying to argue against. This is also not merely an academic debate but leads to political conclusions and outcomes that need to be challenged. For example, labor leader Bill Fletcher Jr., who fits with this tradition of Marxism, wrote against removing police unions from the labor movement during the Black Lives Matter uprisings largely on this "class-first" argument. See Bill Fletcher, Jr., "The Central Issue Is Police Repression, Not Police Unions," *In These Times*, June 12, 2020, http://inthesetimes.com/working/entry/22598/the_central_issue_is_police_repression_not_police_unions.

9. Kimberlé Williams Crenshaw, "Mapping the Margins: Intersectionality,

Identity Politics, and Violence against Women of Color," *Stanford Law Review* 43, 6 (n.d.): 1241–1299. For contemporary uses based on Crenshaw's work, see Ange-Marie Hancock, *Intersectionality: An Intellectual History* (New York: Oxford University Press, 2016); Anna Carastathis, *Intersectionality: Origins, Contestations, Horizons* (Lincoln: University of Nebraska Press, 2016); Patricia Hill Collins and Sirma Bilge, *Intersectionality* (Cambridge, UK: Polity, 2020). For the structure of the law, see Morton J. Horwitz, *The Transformation of American Law, 1780–1860* (Cambridge, Massachusetts: Harvard University Press, 1979).

10. A quick word about class and abstraction. Class is necessarily a social abstraction. In this sense, we could categorize any type of social relationships as a "class." For example, we could analyze politics or history by grouping people into interest blocks based on pet ownership or residence patterns or family structure. Social class as it's defined here is just one possible social form as it relates to economic and cultural factors. But of the possible forms of abstraction, it is a particularly important one. For starters, it is part of a two-hundred-year tradition of people thinking about the defining social relationships under capitalism based on property and wages. As we argue, it is a useful vantage, as it seems to help explain a lot about history and society. But it is not the only one. Additionally, although we make a distinction between material and cultural factors for the purpose of simplification and analysis, it is important to note that this is a conceptual abstraction too and that materiality and culture are fused in lived experience. Things we think of as exclusively economic are shaped by values, conceptions, and practice we may not be aware of. So too for culture, which has important material and structural components. For ideas about the relationship of material and cultural factors, see Pierre Bourdieu, *The Social Structures of the Economy* (Cambridge, United Kingdom: Polity, 2005) and Pierre Bourdieu, "What Makes a Social Class? On the Theoretical and Practical Existence of Groups," *Berkeley Journal of Sociology* 32 (1987): 1–17. Bourdieu's linking of cultural and material factors is generally very useful and in line with our arguments here, but not fully explored in this work. Instead, our concepts of class formation and class composition come from E. P. Thompson and Stuart Hall because their work is more specific to working-class experience. See E. P. Thompson, *The Making of the English Working Class* (New York: Vintage, 1966); Stuart Hall, *Cultural Studies 1983: A Theoretical History*, ed. Jennifer Daryl Slack and Lawrence Grossberg (Durham, North Carolina: Duke University Press, 2016).

11. We argue for a conception of social theory called complementary holism, or intersectionality. In this vision, class is one component of a complex interrelationship of social power. If we stop to look at society or try to understand our world, we find that even the simplest social phenomena are extremely complex. For anyone who cares to look at social problems, isolating any one causal factor in practice or in our analysis is difficult and limiting.

Instead, social problems and events are constructed through a complex web of material and cultural factors and filtered through a variety of lived experiences and understandings. Nevertheless, isolating factors and abstracting from experience can help clarify our thinking and help make the world more known to us. See Michael Albert et al., *Liberating Theory* (Boston: South End Press, 1986); Judith A. Howard, "Intersectionalities," May 29, 2014, http://www.oxfordbibliographies.com/view/document/obo-9780199756384/obo-9780199756384-0111.xml; Crenshaw, "Mapping the Margins."

12. This works takes a "two-class" theory model based on the division of property ownership as its starting point. "Ownership class" we define as access to profitable property. In this, we make the distinction with Proudhon and others between use and possession, and ownership for profit. All our references throughout to property are therefore to profitable ownership, not mere use or possession. See Pierre-Joseph Proudhon, *Proudhon: What Is Property?*, ed. Donald R. Kelley and Bonnie G. Smith (Cambridge, United Kingdom: Cambridge University Press, 1994). There are many on the left now who argue for three- or multiple-class theory in contemporary U.S. society. For example, Michael Albert, Tom Wetzel, and many in the "participatory economics" camp argue for a three-class model in which "intellectuals" and "managers" occupy a third class position that is distinct and can be determinative. Guy Standing has a seven-class model for society. We find these faulty. We agree with Hungarian scholars George Konrad and Ivan Szelenyi that, outside of authoritarian communist societies, where the state acts as a material component of class composition, that intellectuals in "Western" society tend to play a role of a stratum between classes and not a class in themselves. George Konrad and Ivan Szelenyi, *The Intellectuals on the Road to Class Power*, trans. Andrew Arato and Richard E. Allen (New York: Harcourt Brace Jovanovich, 1979); Michael Albert, *Parecon: Life after Capitalism* (London: Verso, 2003); Tom Wetzel, "Workers Power and the Spanish Revolution," December 27, 2006, http://libcom.org/library/workers-power-and-the-spanish-revolution-tom-wetzel. For interesting work exploring the boundaries of class definitions, see Erik Olin Wright, *Class, Crisis, and the State* (London: NLB, 1978). Many works in Erik Olin Wright's career explore this topic.

13. This definition of working-class composition, focused on diversity here, is also true for other classes. However, the main focus of this book is on the working class, not other classes, bourgeois included, and so managerial, precariat, or other class formations will not be considered here.

14. Thompson, *The Making of the English Working Class*, 9; *Voice of Industry*, May 15, 1846, http://industrialrevolution.org/original-issues/1846/1846-05-15.pdf.

15. Douglas Fraser, "Douglas Fraser's Resignation Letter from the Labor-Management Group," http://www.historyisaweapon.com/defcon1/fraserresign.html.

16. David Harvey, *A Brief History of Neoliberalism* (Oxford: Oxford University Press, 2007); Sherry L. Murphy, Jiaquan Xu, Kenneth D. Kochanek, and Elizabeth Arias, "Mortality in the United States, 2017: NCHS Data Brief No. 328, November 2018," https://www.cdc.gov/nchs/products/databriefs/db328 .htm; National Low Income Housing Coalition, "Report Shows African Americans Lost Half Their Wealth Due to Housing Crisis and Unemployment," August 30, 2013, https://nlihc.org/resource/report-shows-african-americans-lost-half -their-wealth-due-housing-crisis-and-unemployment; "The 'Heartbreaking' Decrease in Black Homeownership," *Washington Post*, February 28, 2019, https:// www.washingtonpost.com/news/business/wp/2019/02/28/feature/the -heartbreaking-decrease-in-black-homeownership; Drew Desilver, "For Most U.S. Workers, Real Wages Have Barely Budged in Decades," August 7, 2018, Pew Research Center, https://www.pewresearch.org/fact-tank/2018/08/07/for -most-us-workers-real-wages-have-barely-budged-for-decades; National Women's Law Center, "NWLC Resources on Poverty, Income, and Health Insurance in 2016," September 12, 2017, https://nwlc.org/resources/nwlc-resources-on -poverty-income-and-health-insurance-in-2016.

Chapter 1: Experience

1. Devra Weber, *Dark Sweat, White Gold: California Farm Workers, Cotton, and the New Deal* (Berkeley: University of California Press, 1996), 73.

2. Weber, *Dark Sweat, White Gold*, 63, 73.

3. Weber, *Dark Sweat, White Gold*, 74.

4. "Now I know that some at our colliery that has three or four lads and lasses, and they live one room not half as good as your cellar. I don't pretend to know very much, but I know there shouldn't be that much difference." Thompson, *The Making of the English Working Class*, 715.

5. Thompson, *The Making of the English Working Class*, 772, 829 (the paper expresses these words in an exchange between commentators).

6. Thompson, *The Making of the English Working Class*, 772. It should be noted, however, as Thompson does, that the *Gorgon* also sought individual rather than collective solutions to these problems. Something Thompson does not consider is the nationalist and ethnically homogenous language used by the workers that illustrates racial formation happening at the same time as class formation. This is something we explore further in chapter 5 when discussing the work of Robinson and his ideas about racial capitalism in the English context.

7. Thompson, *The Making of the English Working Class*, 778.

8. Thompson, *The Making of the English Working Class*, 778.

9. Philip Dray, *There Is Power in a Union: The Epic Story of Labor in America* (New York: Doubleday, 2010), 74. We use *sic* here to highlight the use of "men." For minimal disruption of readability we will mark the use in the first instance only.

10. Thompson, *Making*, 822.

11. Thompson, *Making*, 829. This is an important point regarding Leninist ideas that workers are only capable of "trade union consciousness," part of the basis for the theory of the vanguard party. For Lenin, workers were only capable of trade union consciousness, limited vision, and goals that prevented a fundamental critique of capitalism and foreclosed the development of transformative socialist politics. But the ideas expressed from English workers themselves and in many other instances trouble this idea. As we argue here, worker intellectual traditions are often very sophisticated and far-sighted. Sylvis's "permanent antagonism," for example, is a stunning reproach to Lenin's ideas of the limits of trade union consciousness. For more on how English workers were racialized, see Cedric J. Robinson, *Black Marxism: The Making of the Black Radical Tradition* (Chapel Hill: University of North Carolina Press, 2000).

12. Thompson, *Making*, 807, 831, 832.

13. Much of this section is taken from my earlier work. See Michael Reagan, "Band of Sisters: Class and Gender in Industrial Lowell," *Ex Post Facto* 17, no. 1 (2008): 63–90.

14. Bruce Laurie, *Artisans into Workers: Labor in Nineteenth-Century America* (Urbana: University of Illinois Press, 1997); Thomas Dublin, *Women at Work: The Transformation of Work and Community in Lowell, Massachusetts, 1826–1860* (New York: Columbia University Press, 1981); Reagan, "Band of Sisters."

15. Nancy F. Cott, *The Bonds of Womanhood: "Woman's Sphere" in New England, 1780–1835* (New Haven: Yale University Press, 1997).

16. Victoria Bissell Brown and Timothy J. Shannon, eds. "The Question of Female Citizenship: Court Records from the New Nation," in *Going to the Source: The Bedford Reader in American History, Volume 1: To 1877* (Boston: Bedford/St. Martin's, 2004), 9; Jeanne Boydston, *Home and Work: Housework, Wages, and the Ideology of Labor in the Early Republic* (New York: Oxford University Press, 1990), 82.

17. Cott, *Bonds of Womanhood*, 5; Brown and Shannon, "Question of Female Citizenship," 24.

18. Gerda Lerner, "The Lady and the Mill Girl: Changes in the Status of Women in the Age of Jackson," *Midcontinent American Studies Journal* 10, no. 1 (1969), 11–12; Tithi Bhattacharya, *Social Reproduction Theory: Remapping Class, Recentring Oppression* (London: Pluto Press, 2017).

19. Seth Luther, "An Address to the Working Men of New England, on the State of Education, and on the Condition of the Producing Classes in Europe and America," http://hdl.handle.net/2027/nyp.33433007279445?urlappend=%3Bseq=15; Reagan, "Band of Sisters."

20. *Voice of Industry*, January 8, 1847, http://industrialrevolution.org/original-issues/1847/1847-01-08.pdf; Reagan, "Band of Sisters."

21. Sarah Bagley Document Project, "Constitution of the Lowell Factory Girls Association, 1836," http://www.alexanderstreet6.com/wasm; Reagan, "Band of Sisters."

22. *Voice of Industry*, May 15, 1846.

23. Dublin, *Women at Work*; Philip Foner, *Women and the American Labor Movement: From the First Trade Unions to the Present* (New York: Free Press, 1982), 35; Sarah Bagley Document Project, "1846 Ten-Hour Petition to the Massachusetts State Senate," http://www.alexanderstreet6.com/wasm.

24. Harriet H. Robinson, *Loom and Spindle, or Life among the Early Mill Girls* (Kailua, Hawai'i: Press Pacifica, 1976), 51.

25. Dray, *There is Power in a Union*, 26.

Chapter 2: Slavery and Wages

1. See Robinson, *Black Marxism*; Michael Omi, *Racial Formation in the United States* (New York: Routledge, 2014).

2. Edmund S. Morgan, *American Slavery, American Freedom* (New York: W.W. Norton, 2003), 300.

3. Morgan, *American Slavery, American Freedom*, 154; Nikole Hannah-Jones, ed., "The 1619 Project," *New York Times Magazine*, August 14, 2019, https://www.nytimes.com/interactive/2019/08/14/magazine/howard-university-law-school.html.

4. Morgan, *American Slavery, American Freedom*, 319–324.

5. Morgan, *American Slavery, American Freedom*, 308; Elizabeth Sprigs, "'We unfortunate English people suffer here:' An Indentured Servant Writes Home," History Matters, http://historymatters.gmu.edu/d/5796.

6. Morgan, *American Slavery, American Freedom*, 155, 327.

7. Morgan, *American Slavery, American Freedom*, 250.

8. Morgan, *American Slavery, American Freedom*, 270, 328.

9. Morgan, *American Slavery, American Freedom*, 310–314.

10. Morgan, *American Slavery, American Freedom*, 330–336.

11. W. E. Burghardt Du Bois, *Black Reconstruction in America, 1860–1880* (New York: Free Press, 1998); David R. Roediger, *The Wages of Whiteness: Race and the Making of the American Working Class* (London: Verso, 2007).

12. Dray, *There is Power in a Union*, 34, 35. We use *sic* here to highlight the use of "men." For minimal disruption of readability we will mark the use in the first instance only.

13. Dray, *There is Power in a Union*, 35–36.

14. Dray, *There is Power in a Union*, 45.

15. Caitlin Rosenthal, *Accounting for Slavery: Masters and Management* (Cambridge, Massachusetts: Harvard University Press, 2018); Caitlin Rosenthal, "Slavery's Scientific Management: Masters and Managers," in *Slavery's Capitalism: A New History of American Economic Development*, ed. Sven

Beckert and Seth Rockman (Philadelphia: University of Pennsylvania Press, 2016), 62–86; Edward E. Baptist, *The Half Has Never Been Told: Slavery and the Making of American Capitalism* (New York: Basic Books, 2014); Walter Johnson, *River of Dark Dreams: Slavery and Empire in the Cotton Kingdom* (Cambridge, Massachusetts: Belknap Press, 2017).

16. Rosenthal, *Accounting for Slavery*, 4.

17. Baptist, *Half*, 113, 126, 128; Johnson, *River of Dark Dreams*. There are likely many factors that contributed to the increase, among them more productive crop strains. But increased labor productivity is undoubtedly part of the increase.

18. Baptist, *Half*, 134, 121.

19. R. Keith Aufhauser, "Slavery and Scientific Management," *Journal of Economic History* 33, 4 (1973): 811–824.

20. Rosenthal, *Accounting for Slavery*, 143; Baptist, *Half*, 125–126; Henry Wiencek, "The Dark Side of Thomas Jefferson," *Smithsonian Magazine*, October 2012, http://www.smithsonianmag.com/history/the-dark-side-of-thomas-jefferson-35976004.

21. Aufhauser, "Slavery and Scientific Management," 812; Stephen Mihm, "Amazon's Labor-Tracking Wristband Has a History," *Bloomberg*, February 23, 2018, https://www.bloomberg.com/opinion/articles/2018-02-23/amazon-s-labor-tracking-wristband-has-a-rich-history-behind-it; "Digital Taylorism," *Economist*, September 10, 2015, https://www.economist.com/business/2015/09/10/digital-taylorism; Simon Head, "Worse than Wal-Mart: Amazon's Sick Brutality and Secret History of Ruthlessly Intimidating Workers," *Salon*, February 23, 2014, https://www.salon.com/2014/02/23/worse_than_wal_mart_amazons_sick_brutality_and_secret_history_of_ruthlessly_intimidating_workers.

22. Carl Gersuny, "'A Devil in Petticoats' and Just Cause: Patterns of Punishment in Two New England Textile Factories," *Business History Review* 50, no. 2 (1976): 136–137; Caroline F. Ware, *The Early New England Cotton Manufacture: A Study in Industrial Beginnings* (Boston: Houghton Mifflin, 1931), 266. This section is taken from my earlier work; see Reagan, "Band of Sisters," 63–90.

23. Ware, *Early New England Cotton Manufacture*, 266.

24. Gersuny, "Devil in Petticoats," 141, 138; Aufhauser, "Slavery and Scientific Management," 824; Reagan, "Band of Sisters." There is an obvious link to patriarchal systems of control too, and the one record of a working woman whose husband came to fetch her is an obvious example. Again, these forces are intersectional, but we analyze them individually here for the purpose of illustration.

25. Dray, *There is Power in a Union*; Sven Beckert, *The Monied Metropolis: New York City and the Consolidation of the American Bourgeoisie, 1850–1896* (Cambridge, United Kingdom: Cambridge University Press, 2003); Sam Mitrani, *The Rise of the Chicago Police Department: Class and Conflict, 1850–1894*

(Urbana: University of Illinois Press, 2013); Paul Avrich, *The Haymarket Tragedy* (Princeton, New Jersey: Princeton University Press, 1986).

26. Mitrani, *Chicago Police Department*

27. Weber, *Dark Sweat, White Gold*, 148, 150.

28. Joseph E. Lowndes, *From the New Deal to the New Right: Race and the Southern Origins of Modern Conservatism.* (New Haven: Yale University Press, 2008); Ira Katznelson, Kim Geiger, and Daniel Kryder, "Limiting Liberalism: The Southern Veto in Congress, 1933–1950," *Political Science Quarterly* 108, no. 2 (1993), 297; Robert O. Self, *All in the Family: The Realignment of American Democracy since the 1960s* (New York: Hill and Wang, 2013).

29. Honey, *Black Workers Remember*, 95–99.

30. Interview with Lillian Roberts, no date, Bernard Bellush Papers, Robert F. Wagner Labor Archives.

31. Jake Rosenfeld, *What Unions No Longer Do* (Cambridge, Massachusetts: Harvard University Press, 2014), 4, 105, 118, 128, 130; Trevor Griffey, *Black Power's Labor Politics: The United Construction Workers Association and Title VII Law in the 1970s* (PhD diss., University of Washington, 2011).

Chapter 3: Materialism

1. When we say that social relationships are material in "some versions" of class theory, we are drawing on the Marxist analysis that the social relationships of class are "material." However, as we try to show in this book, that is a diminished view of class. Yes, the social relationships of class are material in that they are tied to property, wages, profits, and real material gains. But they are social constructions too, in which the acceptance of the relationship is imagined to be brought into being. See the Chapter 4, "Culture," for a more detailed discussion.

2. John W. Yolton, *The Locke Reader: Selections from the Works of John Locke with a General Introduction and Commentary* (Cambridge, United Kingdom: Cambridge University Press, 1977), 287–295. We use *sic* here to highlight the use of "men." For minimal disruption of readability we will mark the use in the first instance only.

3. Yolton, *Locke Reader*, 287–295.

4. Yolton, *Locke Reader*, 287–295.

5. Wilhelm von Humboldt, *The Limits of State Action* (Indianapolis: Liberty Fund, 1993), 19.

6. Humboldt, *Limits of State Action*, 22.

7. Humboldt, *Limits of State Action*, 24–28. Note the similarities between Humboldt's definition of liberty and ideas later developed by Marx on "alienation."

8. Alexis De Tocqueville, *Democracy in America* (New York: Signet Classics, 2001), 216.

9. Tocqueville, *Democracy in America*, 217.

10. Tocqueville, *Democracy in America*, 217–219.

11. P.J. Proudhon, *What Is Property? An Inquiry into the Principle of Right and of Government*, trans. Benjamin R. Tucker (Princeton, Massachusetts: Benj. R. Tucker, 1876), 11, 45, 150.

12. Proudhon, *What Is Property?*, 223.

13. Proudhon, *What Is Property?*, 123.

14. Proudhon, *What Is Property?*, 112–113.

15. Peter Kropotkin, *The Conquest of Bread* (Montréal: Black Rose Books, 1996), 14, 29–38.

16. Proudhon, *What Is Property?*, 147, 148.

17. Karl Marx, *Capital: A Critique of Political Economy, Vol. 3*, trans. David Fernbach (New York: Penguin Classics, 1993), 1025; Karl Marx and Friedrich Engels, "Manifesto of the Communist Party," in *The Marx-Engels Reader*, ed. Robert C. Tucker (New York: W.W. Norton, 1978), 473 (henceforth *MER*).

18. Marx and Engels, "Economic and Political Manuscripts," in *MER*, 71.

19. Marx and Engels, "Economic and Political Manuscripts," in *MER*, 71.

20. Karl Marx, *Capital: Volume 1: A Critique of Political Economy*, trans. Ben Fowkes (New York: Penguin Classics, 1992), 277; Karl Marx, *Wage-Labour and Capital and Value, Price, and Profit* (New York: International Publishers Co., 1975), 38–39. Perhaps we can forgive Marx here regarding this confusion. The manuscript was never intended for publication and was an early piece of exposition by Marx attempting to clarify his ideas to himself. If we take the concept of alienation and look at Marx's other published works, however, we get no closer to conceptual clarity around the causality of alienation. For example, in *Capital: Volume 1*, Marx seems to write about alienation as an inherent feature of all labor. Because a product's so-called use-value cannot be realized until it is complete, Marx seems to view a worker's alienation from her product as a function of time. In this schema, alienation seems fundamental to any process of labor. However, in an address given to the First International in June 1865 later published as "Value, Price and Profit," in his discussion of the origins of surplus value, Marx seems to indicate that alienation stems from an historical process of "original accumulation," meaning the creation of private property, and the subsequent class divisions that compel workers to sell their labor-power. In this version, the relationship of property, classes, wages, and the like are the origin of a specific type of labor production that includes aspects of alienation. Although the second version seems more in line with Marx's later thinking on materialism, its resolution for our purposes is not that important. Instead, worker alienation seems an integral part of wage labor that explains a lot about current conditions of work, and we argue that the type of alienation found in wage labor is very different from other forms of labor freely undertaken.

21. Marx and Engels, "Economic and Political Manuscripts," in *MER*, 78–80; Marx, *Value, Price, and Profit*, 39.

22. The wages-to-prices relationship has subsequently been called the "transformation" problem in Marxist historiography. It's too complicated to review here, but critics are likely right. Marx's attempt to link all profit accumulation to labor exploitation through price doesn't hold up to rigorous examination. Nonetheless, within the wage, the relation of wages and profits in what Marx classifies as surplus value is a productive insight; in the end, however, this is little more than an elaboration of the labor theory of value. For a productive discussion from a sympathetic vantage, see Jonathan Nitzan and Shimshon Bichler, *Capital as Power: A Study of Order and Creorder* (New York: Routledge, 2009). Another problem here is that profit comes from the exploitation of the natural environment as well. See William Cronon, *Nature's Metropolis: Chicago and the Great West* (New York: W.W. Norton, 1992). For the ongoing impacts of so-called primitive accumulation, see Glen Sean Coulthard, *Red Skin, White Masks: Rejecting the Colonial Politics of Recognition* (Minneapolis: University of Minnesota Press, 2014).

23. Marx, *Capital: Volume 1*, 270; Marx, *Value, Price, and Profit*, 31.

24. Marx, *Capital: Volume 1*, 274–275.

25. Plus other costs.

26. Excluding other costs.

27. Marx, *Value, Price, and Profit*, 40–46. We disagree that reproductive costs set the price of the wage and instead argue that labor markets and collective power determine wages, as we saw with the women of Lowell.

28. Marx, *Value, Price, and Profit*, 40–46.

29. For the problem of quantifying "socially necessary labor-power," see Bob Milward, *Marxian Political Economy: Theory, History, and Contemporary Relevance* (New York: St Martin's Press, 2000). On primitive accumulation as an ongoing process, see Cronon, *Nature's Metropolis*; Silvia Federici, *Caliban and the Witch: Women, the Body and Primitive Accumulation* (New York: Autonomedia, 2004); Coulthard, *Red Skin, White Masks*.

30. Marx's ideas were complex and changed throughout his career, so it's hard to say that the totality of his work was overly determinist. Much of his historical work, for example, draws on social, cultural, and political developments not directly "determined" by class. But in his early writing, and certainly in the thinking of some of his acolytes, this material construction can be very heavily overdrawn. Take for example this selection from the "Contribution to the Critique of Political Economy," published in 1859 and cited by some of the more dogmatic materialists: "In the social production of their existence, men [*sic*] inevitably enter into definite relations, which are independent of their will, namely relations of production appropriate to a given stage in the development of their material forces of production. The totality of these relations of production constitutes the economic structure

of society, the real foundation, on which arises a legal and political super-structure and to which correspond definite forms of social consciousness. The mode of production of material life conditions the general process of social, political and intellectual life. It is not the consciousness of men that determines their existence, but their social existence that determines their consciousness. At a certain stage of development, the material productive forces of society come into conflict with the existing relations of production or—this merely expresses the same thing in legal terms—with the property relations within the framework of which they have operated hitherto. From forms of development of the productive forces these relations turn into their fetters. Then begins an era of social revolution. The changes in the economic foundation lead sooner or later to the transformation of the whole immense superstructure. In studying such transformations it is always necessary to dis-tinguish between the material transformation of the economic conditions of production, which can be determined with the precision of natural science, and the legal, political, religious, artistic or philosophic—in short, ideological forms in which men become conscious of this conflict and fight it out . . . this consciousness must be explained from the contradictions of material life, from the conflict existing between the social forces of production and the relations of production." Marx and Engels, "Contribution to the Critique of Political Economy," in *MER*, 4. This is just one example of many of Marx's overly deterministic writings, the best example of which comes in "The Ger-man Ideology," in which he argues for a very strongly determinist position on materiality and consciousness. See the section "Concerning the Production of Consciousness" and other sections for a fuller discussion. Excerpts from Marx and Engels, "The German Ideology," in *MER*, 146–200. It must also be noted that many of the best Marxists refrain from this framing and have a much more complex vision of social causality. We bring it up here because this framing set the terms of the debate about class for the next century and will be explored in later chapters.

31. See Rudolf Rocker, *Nationalism and Culture* (Facsimile Publisher, 2015).

32. See Marx, *The Eighteenth Brumaire of Louis Bonaparte* (New York: In-ternational Publishers, 1994). On the interplay of material and cultural fac-tors, see Eugene Goodheart, "Is History a Science?," *Philosophy and Literature* 29, no. 2 (2005): 477–488; Bourdieu, *Social Structures* (especially his concept of "habitus"). On the material constructions of race, see N. D. B. Connolly, *A World More Concrete: Real Estate and the Remaking of Jim Crow South Florida* (Chicago: University of Chicago Press, 2016); Keeanga-Yamahtta Taylor, *Race for Profit: How Banks and the Real Estate Industry Undermined Black Home-ownership* (Chapel Hill: University of North Carolina Press, 2019).

Chapter 4: Culture

1. Voltairine de Cleyre and Hippolyte Havel, *Selected Works of Voltairine de Cleyre* (Mother Earth Publishing Association, 1914), 80.

2. As we saw in the previous chapter, Marx's writing at times expressed a very dogged emphasis on the primacy of material factors, although, as we've said, his historical writing is more nuanced. See Marx and Engels, "Contribution to the Critique of Political Economy," in *MER*; Marx, *Eighteenth Brumaire*. See also Aaron Major and the journal *Catalyst* for examples of contemporary Marxists who still advocate this position. Aaron Major, "Ideas Without Power," *Catalyst: A Journal of Theory and Strategy* 2, 3 (Fall 2018), https://catalyst-journal.com/vol2/no3/ideas-without-power. Major is more nuanced, but still comes down on the side of materialism. "Expert ideas, even those emerging from the apolitical depths of academic departments and research centers, are similarly shaped and defined by alignments of material forces," he writes. No doubt true, but they also can take on a life of their own, as we've seen with gender and labor markets already and will explore more fully in this chapter. David Harvey is a particular offender in arguing the primacy of material factors. See David Harvey, *The Condition of Postmodernity: An Enquiry into the Origins of Cultural Change* (Oxford: Wiley-Blackwell, 1991). In this work, he argues that the "epiphenomenon" of postmodernism, including art, architecture, and academic theory, was caused by the financialization of the economy and its impacts on the social function of time. Although many other Marxists are much better on this question, there are many more examples of "orthodox" Marxists who reject cultural causality.

3. Eduard Bernstein, *Bernstein: The Preconditions of Socialism* (Cambridge, United Kingdom: Cambridge University Press, 1993). Bernstein is a complex figure, and on many counts we disagree with his ideas and political practice. But there is merit to his critique of dogmatic materialism, as we explore here.

4. Bernstein, *Bernstein: Preconditions*, 14.

5. Bernstein, *Bernstein: Preconditions*, 18. Bernstein was critiqued for other notions, and with greater cause. For example, Bernstein became a leading exponent of gradualist class reforms within the capitalist state. Indeed, revolutionaries we very much admire, such as Rosa Luxembourg and others, vigorously and viciously condemned Bernstein for this. Her polemic, "Reform or Revolution," was a response to Bernstein and a rather brilliant defense of revolutionary strategy against the accomodationist perspective of Bernstein.

6. Warlaam Tcherkesoff, *Pages of Socialist History: Teachings and Acts of Social Democracy* (New York: C. B. Cooper, 1902), 13–14, 78.

7. Rocker, *Nationalism and Culture*, 10–22.

8. Rocker, *Nationalism and Culture*, 10–22.

9. Rocker, *Nationalism and Culture*, 10–22.

10. Rocker, *Nationalism and Culture*, 10–22. We use *sic* here to highlight the use of "men." For minimal disruption of readability we will mark the use

in the first instance only.

11. Rocker, *Nationalism and Culture*, 10–22.

12. E. P. Thompson, *Poverty of Theory* (New York: Monthly Review Press, 1978).

13. Thompson, *Poverty of Theory*, 5–9.

14. Thompson, *Poverty of Theory*, 5–9.

15. We're thinking here of Marx's opening to *The Eighteenth Brumaire of Louis Bonaparte*, in which he writes that "men make their own history, but they do not make it just as they please; they do not make it under circumstances chosen by themselves, but under circumstance directly encountered, given and transmitted from the past. The tradition of all the dead generations weighs like a nightmare on the brain of the living." Not just this quote, but Marx's historical and empirical arguments throughout the *Eighteenth Brumaire* is some of his strongest work in this regard. Marx, *Eighteenth Brumaire*, 15.

16. See Perry Anderson, *Arguments within English Marxism* (London: Verso, 1980); Cohen, *Marx's Theory of History*; Leiman, *Political Economy of Racism*; and even Hall, *Cultural Studies 1983*.

17. Thompson, *Poverty of Theory*, 188–192.

18. Thompson, *Making*, 9–11.

19. Thompson, *Making*, 9–11.

20. Hall, *Cultural Studies 1983*, 34, 46. See also Hall, "Rethinking the 'Base and Superstructure' Metaphor," in which he argues Marx himself was forced to "break" with the dogmatic version of economic determinism from his earlier writings. Stuart Hall, "Rethinking the 'Base and Superstructure' Metaphor," in *Essential Essays, Volume 1: Foundations of Cultural Studies*, ed. David Morley (Durham, North Carolina: Duke University Press, 2019).

21. Hall, *Cultural Studies 1983*, 110. A common Marxist rebuttal here is that class dynamics and relations of class power, part of the economic base, are what ultimately caused the passage of the Acts. And this is true, of course, but our Marxist comrades miss the point. This is an example of law (the superstructure) affecting the material relations of production. Once the laws are in place and enforced, they become part of social and cultural expectations of society, and they affect the very structure of material factors, restricting market access for children, for example. The point here is that historical causality is complex. It's not that class relations and economic force play no role; they do, and so too do culture, consciousness, law, and other aspects of social organization. For a truly excellent study with an emphasis on culture looking at exactly this complication in the case of child labor laws in the United States, see Viviana A. Zelizer, *Pricing the Priceless Child: The Changing Social Value of Children* (Princeton, New Jersey: Princeton University Press, 1994). See also Hall's discussion of Marx and the law in "Rethinking the 'Base and Superstructure' Metaphor" in *Essential Essays, Volume 1*, 157.

22. John Scott, "Structure," in *A Dictionary of Sociology*, ed. John Scott (Oxford: Oxford University Press, 2015); Daniel Chandler and Rod Munday, "Social Structure," in *A Dictionary of Media and Communication* (Oxford: Oxford University Press, 2016).

23. Hall, *Cultural Studies 1983*, 54–73.

24. Benjamin Lee Whorf, *Language, Thought, and Reality: Selected Writings of Benjamin Lee Whorf*, ed. John B. Carroll (Cambridge, Massachusetts: MIT Press, 1964); Paul J. Thibault, "Whorf, Benjamin Lee," in *Encyclopedia of Semiotics* (Oxford: Oxford University Press, 2007).

25. Hall, *Cultural Studies 1983*, 122.

26. Hall, *Cultural Studies 1983*, 122.

27. Hall, *Cultural Studies 1983*, 122.

28. Hall, *Cultural Studies 1983*, 144–145.

29. Hall, *Cultural Studies 1983*, 146–153. See also his "What Is This 'Black' in Black Popular Culture?" for his discussion of how culture is a "space of contestation" specifically focused on the question of the signification of "Black." Stuart Hall, *Essential Essays, Volume 2: Identity and Diaspora*, ed. David Morley (Durham, North Carolina: Duke University Press Books, 2019), 85. Here Hall is very explicitly drawing on the work of Marxist theorist Antonio Gramsci, an early developer of the notion of cultural struggle. See Antonio Gramsci, *Selections from the Prison Notebooks*, eds. Quintin Hoare and Geoffrey Nowell Smith (New York: International Publishers, 1971).

30. Stephanie M. H. Camp, "Black Is Beautiful: An American History," *Journal of Southern History* 81, no. 3 (August 2015): 675–690; Maxine B. Craig, "Black Is Beautiful: Personal Transformation and Political Change," (PhD diss., University of California at Berkeley, 1995); Susannah Walker, "Black Is Profitable: The Commodification of the Afro, 1960–1975," *Enterprise and Society* 1, no. 3 (2000): 536–564.

31. Angela Y. Davis, "Afro Images: Politics, Fashion, and Nostalgia," *Critical Inquiry* 21, no. 1 (1994): 37–45; Robin D. G. Kelley, "Nap Time: Historicizing the Afro," *Fashion Theory* 1, no. 4 (1997): 339–351.

Chapter 5: Intersectionality

1. "The Combahee River Collective Statement," *Ms.* 2, no. 1 (1991): 40. The idea of "intersectionality" has been critiqued from a number of perspectives, many of them academic. Most of the criticisms attempt to trouble the metaphor of intersectionality by asking questions about how individual forms of social power "intersect" or about what exists outside the point of intersection. These critiques miss the mark by taking the metaphor too literally. Intersectional theory is useful in an abstract way to think about how systems of social power that we may think of as distinct in fact work to reinforce one another. Although we prefer the language of "complementary holism" to

approximate the same idea, we also like the language of intersectionality to grapple with similar concepts, and it has become the dominant language to express these ideas. See also Albert et al., *Liberating Theory*.

2. "Combahee River Collective Statement."

3. Robin D. G. Kelley, "Cedric J. Robinson: The Making of a Black Radical Intellectual," June 17, 2016, http://www.counterpunch.org/2016/06/17/cedric-j-robinson-the-making-of-a-black-radical-intellectual.

4. Robinson, *Black Marxism*, 2.

5. Robinson, *Black Marxism*, 66.

6. Robinson, *Black Marxism*, 39.

7. Robinson, *Black Marxism*, xxx.

8. Du Bois, *Black Reconstruction*, 55–83.

9. Du Bois, *Black Reconstruction*, 670–710.

10. Eric Foner, *Give Me Liberty! An American History, Vol. 1* (New York: W. W. Norton, 2011), 594.

11. C. L. R. James, Raya Dunayevskaya, and Paul Buhle, *State Capitalism & World Revolution* (Chicago: Charles H. Kerr, 1986); C. L. R. James, *The Black Jacobins: Toussaint L'Ouverture and the San Domingo Revolution* (New York: Vintage, 1989).

12. C. L. R. James, "J. R. Johnson: The Historical Development of the Negroes in American Society (December 1943)," July 2015, https://www.marxists.org/archive/james-clr/works/1943/negro43.htm. Thanks to Wayne Price for this resource.

13. Frantz Fanon, *The Wretched of the Earth* (New York: Grove, 1968), 40. See also the excellent introduction in Coulthard, *Red Skin, White Masks*. Hall points out that the specific articulation that Fanon creates here might be over drawn. In particular circumstances, articulations, there might be a direct, causal correlation of the type that Fanon makes between whiteness and class. In others, it might be more complicated, with different articulations of race, class, and gender taking on different meaning and different structural form. Hall, *Cultural Studies 1983*, 146.

14. Katznelson, Geiger, and Kryder, "Limiting Liberalism," 283–306.

15. Michael K. Honey, *Going Down Jericho Road: The Memphis Strike, Martin Luther King's Last Campaign* (New York: W.W. Norton & Company, 2008); Michael K. Honey, *To the Promised Land: Martin Luther King and the Fight for Economic Justice*, (New York: W. W. Norton, 2018).

16. Nancy MacLean, *Freedom Is Not Enough: The Opening of the American Workplace* (Cambridge, Massachusetts: Harvard University Press, 2008), 5.

17. Bhattacharya, *Social Reproduction Theory*.

18. Selma James and Mariarosa Dalla Costa, "The Power of Women and the Subversion of the Community," in Selma James, Nina Lopez, and Marcus Rediker, *Sex, Race and Class—The Perspective of Winning: A Selection of Writings 1952–2011* (Oakland: PM Press, 2012).

19. James and Dalla Costa, "Power of Women."

20. Boydston, *Home and Work*; Gus Wezerek and Kristen R. Ghodsee, "Women's Unpaid Labor Is Worth $10,900,000,000,000," *New York Times*, March 5, 2020, https://www.nytimes.com/interactive/2020/03/04/opinion/women-unpaid-labor.html; James et al., *Sex, Race and Class*, 93.

21. James and Dalla Costa, "Power of Women," 51. The idea of the social factory originally came from Italian Autonomist Marxists. See David Palazzo, "The 'Social Factory' in Postwar Italian Radical Thought from Operaismo to Autonomia" (PhD diss., City University of New York, 2014).

22. James and Dalla Costa, "Power of Women," 51. For more, see Catharine A. MacKinnon, *Toward a Feminist Theory of the State* (Cambridge, Massachusetts: Harvard University Press, 1989).

23. Dorothy Sue Cobble, *The Other Women's Movement: Workplace Justice and Social Rights in Modern America* (Princeton, New Jersey: Princeton University Press, 2004), 7–8.

24. Federici, *Caliban and the Witch*, 16.

25. Federici, *Caliban and the Witch*, 14.

26. Federici, *Caliban and the Witch*, 163–173.

27. Anonymous, "The Combahee River Collective Statement."

28. Sojourner Truth, "Ain't I a Woman?" Fordham University, Modern History Sourcebooks, December 1851, https://sourcebooks.fordham.edu/mod/sojtruth-woman.asp. See also, "The Sojourner Truth Project," https://www.thesojournertruthproject.com.

29. Truth, "Ain't I a Woman?"

30. Angela Y. Davis, *Women, Race, and Class* (New York: Vintage, 1983).

31. Davis, *Women, Race, and Class*.

32. Collins, *Black Feminist Thought*, 32.

33. Collins, *Black Feminist Thought*, 40.

34. Howard Zinn, *A People's History of the United States* (New York: Harper Perennial Modern Classics, 2005), 253.

Chapter 6: Practice

1. Merle Goldman, "Hu Yaobang's Intellectual Network and the Theory Conference of 1979," *China Quarterly* 126 (June 1991): 219–242; Michael Schoenhals, "The 1978 Truth Criterion Controversy," *China Quarterly*, 126 (1991): 243–268. Hu was a Communist Party member and revolutionary in the 1930s but went on to become a leading figure of reform following the death of Mao. His 1978 article was a touchstone of reform efforts in China and largely used by Deng to bring about Chinese state capitalism, or "socialism with Chinese characteristics," as it's known there. But Hu also supported reform efforts of popular sectors of the Chinese working class. For example, in 1987, he supported student protests, a move that cost him his job. When

he died in 1989, student mourners took to Tiananmen Square in memorial, leading to the uprising and massacre. Although the demonstrators, and by association Hu, are seen as pro-capitalist democracy reformers, the reality is more complicated, as Hu maintained a commitment to anti-capitalist economics with more popular democratic participation.

2. Du Bois, *Black Reconstruction.*

3. Institute for Industrial Education, *The Durban Strikes 1973: "--- Human Being with Souls ---"* (Durban: Institute for Industrial Education, 1974); Peter Cole, *Dockworker Power: Race and Activism in Durban and the San Francisco Bay Area* (Urbana: University of Illinois Press, 2018); South African History Online, "1973 Durban Strikes," https://www.sahistory.org.za/article/1973-durban-strikes. It is perhaps not surprising that Robinson first encountered the term "racial capitalism" in reference to South Africa's systems of exploitation and oppression.

4. David Brody, *Labor in Crisis: The Steel Strike of 1919* (Urbana: University of Illinois Press, 1965).

5. Michael Goldfield, "Race and the CIO: The Possibilities for Racial Egalitarianism during the 1930s and 1940s," *International Labor and Working-Class History*, 44 (1993): 1–32.

6. Goldfield, "Race and the CIO," 2. This is not to say the unions were somehow free from racism—far from it. Most of the history of unions in the United States is of institutions supporting white supremacy. However, this type of organizing shows us a way forward and a living tradition from the past. Indeed, partially, and in starts, overcoming racism was the only way the labor movement in the United States could move forward. And workers did it by explicitly targeting racism as a sphere of struggle and highlighting the voices and special struggles of Black workers, not by subsuming Black struggle into the labor struggle. See Griffey, *Black Power's Labor Politics.*

7. Michelle Alexander, *The New Jim Crow: Mass Incarceration in the Age of Colorblindness* (New York: New Press, 2012).

8. German Lopez, "America's Prisoners Are Going on Strike in at Least 17 States," *Vox*, August 17, 2018, https://www.vox.com/2018/8/17/17664048/national-prison-strike-2018; Incarcerated Workers Organizing Committee, "Prison Strike 2018," June 19, 2018, https://incarceratedworkers.org/campaigns/prison-strike-2018.

9. Keeanga-Yamahtta Taylor, *From #BlackLivesMatter to Black Liberation* (Chicago: Haymarket Books, 2016).

10. Taylor, *From #BlackLivesMatter to Black Liberation.*

11. Sarah Jaffe, "The Women of Wages for Housework," *Nation*, March 14, 2018, https://www.thenation.com/article/wages-for-houseworks-radical-vision; Silvia Federici, "Wages against Housework," in Silvia Federici, *Revolution at Point Zero: Housework, Reproduction, and Feminist Struggle* (Oakland: PM Press, 2012).

12. Roderick A. Ferguson, *One-Dimensional Queer* (Medford, Massachusetts: Polity, 2018), 21; Working Class History, "E25-26: The Stonewall Riots and Pride at 50," May 13, 2019, https://workingclasshistory.com/2019/05/13/e21-22-the-stonewall-riots-and-pride-at-50. There is some debate about the appropriateness of using the word "trans" to describe the Stonewall movement. We make use of it despite the different meanings of "trans" in 1969 to reflect the development of movement conceptions of freedom and practice of intersectional organizing.

13. Quotes from Ferguson, *One-Dimensional Queer*, 21, 35; Dean Spade, *Normal Life: Administrative Violence, Critical Trans Politics, and the Limits of Law* (Durham, North Carolina: Duke University Press, 2015); Merle Woo, "Now We Need a Revolution," in Tommi Avicolli Mecca, *Smash the Church, Smash the State!: The Early Years of Gay Liberation* (San Francisco: City Lights Books, 2009).

14. Sarah Lazare, "HR Has Never Been on the Side of Workers. #MeToo Is More Proof," *In These Times*, January 8, 2018, https://inthesetimes.com/article/human-resources-me-too-sexual-harassment-workers-union-labor-ford; Jillian Kestler-D'Amours, "Women in Low-Wage US Farm Jobs Say #MeToo," Al Jazeera, December 12, 2017, https://www.aljazeera.com/news/2017/12/happened-women-wage-jobs-metoo-171204161209204.html.

15. Elia Gran, "How Spain Pulled Off a Women's General Strike," March 20, 2018, https://indypendent.org/2018/03/how-spain-pulled-off-a-womens-general-strike. Some have critiqued the action for not technically being a strike; see Marianne Garneau, "The Women's Strike, Reconsidered," March 5, 2019, http://organizing.work/2019/03/the-womens-strike-reconsidered; Marianne Garneau, "Guest Podcast on the Women's Strike," March 25, 2019, http://organizing.work/2019/03/guest-podcast on the womens-strike.

16. Bree Busk, "Chile's Feminists Inspire a New Era of Social Struggle," January 28, 2019, http://blackrosefed.org/chile-feminists-new-social-struggle.

17. Pablo Abufom, "Los Seis Meses Que Transformaron Chile," March 4, 2020, http://anarkismo.net/article/31771?search_text=actores+sociales+sector; Busk, "Chile's Feminists."

18. Busk, "Chile's Feminists"; Alisha Holl, "Chile's Streets Are Filled with Protests. How Did a 4 Percent Fare Hike Set off Such Rage?," *Washington Post*, November 1, 2019, https://www.washingtonpost.com/politics/2019/11/01/chiles-streets-are-fire-with-protests-how-did-percent-fare-hike-set-off-such-rage.

19. Escuela de Cuadros, "Raúl Zibechi: Poder Popular," March 31, 2014, *YouTube*, 34:16, https://www.youtube.com/watch?v=anWMdkF_XZM&feature=youtu.be.

20. Joel Beinin, *Workers and Thieves: Labor Movements and Popular Uprisings in Tunisia and Egypt* (Stanford, California: Stanford University Press, 2015), 105.

21. Beinin, *Workers and Thieves*, 95, 109; Anne Alexander and Mostafa Bassiouny, *Bread, Freedom, Social Justice: Workers and the Egyptian Revolution* (London: Zed Books, 2014).

22. Beinin, *Workers and Thieves*, 95, 109.

23. Walter J. Nicholls, *The Immigrant Rights Movement: The Battle over National Citizenship* (Stanford, California: Stanford University Press, 2019).

24. Theresa Moran, "Behind the Chicago Teachers Strike," *Labor Notes*, September 10, 2012, https://labornotes.org/2012/09/behind-chicago-teachers-strike; Samantha Winslow, "Chicago Teachers to Strike for Public Schools and Services," *Labor Notes*, March 24, 2016, https://www.labornotes.org/2016/03/chicago-teachers-strike-public-schools-and-services; Barbara Madeloni, "Chicago Teachers Go Out on Strike Again," *Labor Notes*, October 17, 2019, https://www.labornotes.org/2019/10/chicago-teachers-go-out-strike-again.

25. Ellen Brait, "Portland's Bridge-Hangers and 'kayaktivists' Claim Win in Shell Protest," *Guardian*, July 31, 2015, https://www.theguardian.com/business/2015/jul/31/portland-bridge-shell-protest-kayaktivists-fennica-reaction; Caitlyn McClure, "Indigenous Water Protectors Are about to Get Their Revenge on Big Oil," September 3, 2017, https://other98.com/kinder-morgans-tar-sands-pipeline-become-new-dapl; Sam Levin, "Dakota Access Pipeline: The Who, What and Why of the Standing Rock Protests," *Guardian*, November 3, 2016, https://www.theguardian.com/us-news/2016/nov/03/north-dakota-access-oil-pipeline-protests-explainer; Masha Gessen, "The Fifteen-Year-Old Climate Activist Who Is Demanding a New Kind of Politics," *New Yorker*, October 2, 2018, https://www.newyorker.com/news/our-columnists/the-fifteen-year-old-climate-activist-who-is-demanding-a-new-kind-of-politics; Zoë Ducklow, "Nine Things You Need to Know about the Unist'ot'en Blockade," *The Tyee*, January 8, 2019, https://thetyee.ca/Analysis/2019/01/08/LNG-Pipeline-Unistoten-Blockade. Indeed, the pipeline campaigns of Standing Rock and the 2020 Indigenous uprising in Canada demonstrate the crucial links between capital and colonialism present since Locke. See Nick Estes and Jaskiran Dhillon, eds., *Standing with Standing Rock: Voices from the #NoDAPL Movement* (Minneapolis: University of Minnesota Press, 2019). For a theoretical grounding, see Coulthard, *Red Skin, White Masks*.

26. Judi Bari, *Timber Wars* (Monroe, Maine: Common Courage Press, 1994); Graham Purchase, *Anarchism and Ecology* (Montreal: Black Rose Books, 1997).

27. Naomi Klein, *This Changes Everything: Capitalism Vs. The Climate* (New York: Simon & Schuster, 2014).

28. Ronald Magden, *A History of Seattle Waterfront Workers, 1884–1934* (International Longshoremen's and Warehousemen's Union 19 of Seattle, the Washington Commission for the Humanities, 1991); Rod Palmquist, "Labor's Great War on the Seattle Waterfront: A History of the 1934 Longshore Strike,"

NOTES · 193

https://depts.washington.edu/dock/34strikehistory_intro.shtml.

29. Donny Gluckstein, *The Paris Commune: A Revolution in Democracy* (Chicago: Haymarket Books, 2011).

30. Hellen Keller, "Strike against War," in Howard Zinn and Anthony Arnove, *Voices of a People's History of the United States* (New York: Seven Stories Press, 2011), 285.

31. Rosa Luxembourg and Karl Liebnecht were among those killed. Gabriel Kuhn, *All Power to the Councils!: A Documentary History of the German Revolution of 1918–1919* (Oakland: PM Press, 2012).

32. Alexander Rabinowitch, *The Bolsheviks Come to Power: The Revolution of 1917 in Petrograd* (Chicago: Haymarket Books, 2017); Oskar Anweiler, *The Soviets: The Russian Workers, Peasants, and Soldiers Councils, 1905–1921* (New York: Pantheon Books, 1975); Leon Trotsky, *History of the Russian Revolution* (Chicago: Haymarket Books, 2008); Maurice Brinton, *For Workers' Power*, ed. David Goodway (Oakland: AK Press, 2004).

33. Vernon Richards and David Goodway, *Lessons of the Spanish Revolution: 1936–1939* (Oakland: PM Press, 2019); Gaston Leval and Pedro García-Guirao, *Collectives in the Spanish Revolution*, trans. Vernon Richards (Oakland: PM Press, 2018); Martha Ackelsberg, *Free Women of Spain: Anarchism and the Struggle for the Emancipation of Women* (Oakland: AK Press, 2004).

34. Eric Foner, *Give Me Liberty!*

35. Daniel Singer, *Prelude to Revolution: France in May 1968* (Chicago: Haymarket Books, 2013).

Conclusion: On Hope and Solidity

1. Selma James, Nina Lopez, and Marcus Rediker, *Sex, Race and Class—The Perspective of Winning: A Selection of Writings 1952–2011* (Oakland: PM Press, 2012), 95.

2. Federici, *Caliban and the Witch*, 17.

3. Selma James and Mariarosa Dalla Costa, "Power of Women," 19.

4. JOMO has a rather ingenious formulation of this relation: "When queers are discriminated [against] in the hiring process for being too gender deviant, too campy, too out, it is because we jarringly disrupt the capitalist fantasy of a brainless, emotionless, machine-like worker. We are punished for showing that there really isn't a division between the public life in the workplace, and our private lives as sexual, emotional, gendered beings. We bring our private lives into our public lives, the workplace, either because we have no intention or no way to hide who we are." See JOMO, "Queer Liberation Is Class Struggle," January 8, 2010, http://unityandstruggle.org/2010/01/08/queer-liberation-is-class-struggle. On trans activism and intersectional struggle and solidarity, see also Spade, *Normal Life*; Ferguson, *One-Dimensional Queer*.

5. Tcherkesoff, *Pages of Socialist History*, 28.

6. Tcherkesoff, *Pages of Socialist History*, 28.

7. Frances Fox Piven and Richard Cloward, *Poor People's Movements: Why They Succeed, How They Fail* (New York: Vintage, 1978).

8. Vladimir Ilyich Lenin, *Essential Works of Lenin: "What Is to Be Done?" and Other Writings* (New York: Dover Publications, 1987): James, López, and Rediker, *Sex, Race and Class*, 100.

9. DoVeanna S. Fulton, "'There Is Might in Each': Slave Narratives and Black Feminism," in John Ernest, ed., *The Oxford Handbook of the African American Slave Narrative* (Oxford: Oxford University Press, 2014).

Index

Institute for Anarchist Studies

The Institute for Anarchist Studies (IAS) was founded in 1996 and seeks to further antiauthoritarian thought by supporting the work of radical writers, filmmakers, and podcasters. We offer editorial mentorship, working closely with new and established writers to develop their ideas and voices for a general audience, as well as online and print publication opportunities: our website and social media presence; our annual journal, *Perspectives on Anarchist Theory*; and our various book series (published in partnership with AK Press). We also sponsor speakers, performances, and theory tracks at conferences and other public events. We fund leftist thinkers and culture makers, and prioritize creators of minority identities and those who operate outside of academia and therefore have less access to intellectual or material resources. When possible, we give grants to promote work that could not otherwise be made.

For more about the IAS, visit: anarchiststudies.org.

.

AK PRESS is small, in terms of staff and resources, but we also manage to be one of the world's most productive anarchist publishing houses. We publish close to twenty books every year, and distribute thousands of other titles published by like-minded independent presses and projects from around the globe. We're entirely worker run and democratically managed. We operate without a corporate structure—no boss, no managers, no bullshit.

The **FRIENDS OF AK PRESS** program is a way you can directly contribute to the continued existence of AK Press, and ensure that we're able to keep publishing books like this one! Friends pay $25 a month directly into our publishing account ($30 for Canada, $35 for international), and receive a copy of every book AK Press publishes for the duration of their membership! Friends also receive a discount on anything they order from our website or buy at a table: 50% on AK titles, and 30% on everything else. We have a Friends of AK ebook program as well: $15 a month gets you an electronic copy of every book we publish for the duration of your membership. *You can even sponsor a very discounted membership for someone in prison.*

Email **friendsofak@akpress.org** for more info, or visit the website: **https://www.akpress.org/friends.html**.

There are always great book projects in the works—so sign up now to become a Friend of AK Press, and let the presses roll!